INSIDE THE MIND OF
PRESIDENT BIDEN

HS Press

INSIDE THE MIND OF
PRESIDENT BIDEN

**THOUGHTS
REVEALED BY
HIS GUARDIAN SPIRIT
DAYS BEFORE
HIS INAUGURATION**

RYUHO OKAWA

HS PRESS

Copyright © 2021 by Ryuho Okawa
English translation © Happy Science 2021
Original title: *Biden Shugorei no Reigen
-Daitoryo Shunin Chokuzen no Honshin o Kataru-*
HS Press is an imprint of IRH Press Co., Ltd.
Tokyo
ISBN 13: 978-1-943928-02-6
ISBN 10: 1-943928-02-9
Cover Image: AFP=jiji

No statements made by the guardian spirit of Mr. Joseph Biden in this book reflect statements actually made by himself.

The opinions of the spirit in this book do not necessarily reflect those of Happy Science Group.
For the mechanism behind spiritual messages, see the end section.

Contents

Preface 13

CHAPTER ONE

Inside the Mind of President Biden a Week Before the Inauguration

A Spiritual Interview with Mr. Biden's Guardian Spirit—Part 1

1 **The Guardian Spirit of Mr. Biden Suddenly Appeared at Night**

    He appeared to be in pain and revealed who he is 18

    He pleads for Happy Science to give him a spiritual interview 25

2 **Looking Back at the Confusion of the US Presidential Election**

    He says China doesn't matter to him because it's on the other side of the Earth 29

    He believes that Mr. Trump led America to "insanity" 34

    He appeared today to seek a fair interview to voice his views 36

    Mr. Biden's guardian spirit seeks a spiritual interview before the inauguration 40

    His view that Hillary Clinton should have become president before him 44

3 A Look at the Religious Beliefs of Biden's Guardian Spirit

His view that you can win by siding with what's "scientific" 47

He compares Mr. Trump with the jealous god of ancient Israel 49

He's trying to purchase masks from China to foster a closer relationship with Beijing 51

He thinks that Happy Science is a New Age movement 54

He speaks about his past-life relationship with Barack Obama 58

Biden's guiding spirit will probably be similar to Jimmy Carter's guiding spirit 62

4 How Does President Biden Plan to Deal with the Coronavirus Crisis?

Biden wants to deport Trump from the country 67

Why Biden doesn't want to investigate whether Beijing's scheme is behind the coronavirus crisis 71

He says that Biden will press the missile-launch button if everyone tells him to 75

Why Biden's guardian spirit can speak Japanese 78

What will he do if he can't stop the coronavirus' spread after succeeding Trump? 81

He wants to keep the US–Beijing joint research on the coronavirus from getting exposed 84

5 **Looking Into the Character of Mr. Biden, the President-Elect**

The way he views China's surveillance society and the crisis in Hong Kong 88

He believes the mass media hates Trump because he "responds by badmouthing about them" 93

Said in a "positive" way, Biden is someone favorable to Japanese people's tastes 97

He says Trump is a "magician" who enchants people 99

To acquire the market of 1.4 billion Chinese people he wants to avoid ruining relations with Beijing 102

6 **How Biden's Guardian Spirit Considers the Role of America's President**

He imagines the role of America's president as just an honorary one 108

He says that it's good for a simpleton to become the president 114

Will America be able to stop Beijing's evil from now on? 119

Biden's guardian spirit fears getting assassinated 124

He'll listen to everyone else's opinions when he becomes the president 127

CHAPTER TWO

How President Biden Will Deal with Critical Global Issues

*A Spiritual Interview with
Mr. Biden's Guardian Spirit—Part 2*

1 **A Look Inside the Mind of Mr. Biden**

Looking into Biden's true character and thinking to forecast the coming four-year course of the world 134

Mr. Biden's guardian spirit gets summoned and speaks his real thoughts 136

2 **Mr. Biden's State of Mind Shortly Before the Inaugural Ceremony**

Biden's guardian spirit gets summoned and appears 137

He thinks that Trump is like King Kong 140

He says that Kamala Harris was chosen just to gather votes from women and Black people 142

His view on foreign diplomacy is that as many people as possible should be friends 144

The reason he showed support for LGBT people 147

3 **Finding Out His Strategy Against China**

He's planning to negotiate with China enough to avoid war 149

He says there's no use in investigating the real source of the coronavirus 152

Looking at how much he knows about where the coronavirus came from 156

He insists on starting discussions regarding the mass massacres in Uyghur from a blank slate	160
He reveals that the coronavirus research started in the US	162
He is planning on developing mutually supportive diplomatic negotiations with China	165
He will let Japan and China compete in a "sumo match" and will take the winner's side	167
He doesn't see that it's possible for China to gain hegemonic control	172

4 Asking Him about Coronavirus Measures and Environmental Issues

He believes that the coronavirus is a "god of good luck" that drove out Trump	175
His idea of a coronavirus measure is the use of masks, disinfectants, and vaccines	177
Taxes from the wealthy class and large corporations will fund his 2-trillion dollar coronavirus measure	179
He will drive Trump to the point of needing to sell the Trump Tower	182
He believes that investing in environmental preservation won't lead to a great depression	185

5 On Peace in Asia and His Value Judgments on Justice

He thinks that it's only natural for Hong Kong to be eventually assimilated by China	190
He feels that putting pressure on Beijing is enough to handle the genocide in Uyghur	193

He says that he can't intervene into other countries' domestic affairs past a certain line	196
His basic way of thinking regarding defending Taiwan	198
His value judgment on the battle between democracy and totalitarianism	203
Mr. Biden's guardian spirit calls Mr. Trump a "crazy person"	206
He believes that the Senkaku Islands issue and the Japanese constitution's revision are Japan's responsibilities	210

6   Asking Biden's Guardian Spirit about His Vision of the World

On his stance on Iran–Israel issues	214
He warns that Japan should fear more about Russia's possible assault on Hokkaido	220
If China grows, he'll extract as much money from it as he can	223
He mentions that a peculiar person is the determiner of America's justice	225
He says that the president of America has enough power to destroy the planet	228
What he thinks of Kamala Harris and Hillary Clinton	231
He foresees competition between GAFA	237

7   What Will Biden's Presidency Bring to America?

Biden's guardian spirit appears to be full of energy at this time, unlike during the last spiritual interview	240
Biden's guardian spirit feels like Lincoln when he won the Civil War	243

His value judgment is that he'll always take the side of the larger population and higher G.D.P. ... 246

He believes that information about space beings should just be handled by NASA ... 249

He says that Happy Science will survive if they praise him ... 252

Will the world go in the righteous direction under President Biden? ... 257

8 **On President Biden's Character That We Saw in This Spiritual Interview** ... 261

Afterword ... 265

About the Author ... 267

What Is El Cantare? ... 268

What Is a Spiritual Message? ... 270

About Happy Science ... 274

About Happy Science Movies ... 278

About Happiness Realization Party ... 280

Happy Science Academy Junior and Senior High School ... 281

Contact Information ... 282

About IRH Press ... 284

Books by Ryuho Okawa ... 285

Music by Ryuho Okawa ... 295

Preface

Inside this book are the interviews with the guardian spirit of the new president of the United States, Mr. Biden. Both of them were held shortly before the inauguration when he was filled with apprehension about safely getting through the inaugural ceremony and Mr. Biden's subconscious mind was wavering sensitively.

I will let you read the contents, but the following is my impression of him.

My conclusion is that he is a great ordinary person.

Meaning, America chose to elect an ordinary person.

Is there such a shortage of capable people there that they could only choose someone of the fifth dimension—the World of Goodness—as their president? Or it must mean that the views of the people who gather to GAFA and major mass media companies are of that level.

The strongest country in the world has set sail upon a mud boat for the next age. The fall of the nation is coming in the name of "strategic patience." Later generations shall correctly tell about Mr. Trump who cried repeatedly to "Make America Great Again."

Ryuho Okawa
Master and CEO of Happy Science Group
January 29, 2021

CHAPTER ONE

Inside the Mind of President Biden a Week Before the Inauguration

*A Spiritual Interview with
Mr. Biden's Guardian Spirit—Part 1*

*Originally recorded in Japanese on January 13, 2021,
at the Special Lecture Hall of Happy Science in Japan
and later translated into English*

Joseph Robinette Biden, Jr. (1942 - Present)

Joseph Biden is an American politician and a member of the Democratic Party. He is the 46th president of the United States. He was born in Pennsylvania, has graduated from the University of Delaware, and has acquired his law degree at Syracuse University. At the age of 29, he became a US senator in 1972 for the first time and went on to serve six terms in the Senate. In his first presidential run in 1988, he withdrew from the race because he plagiarized a speech by a British member of parliament. Then, he was defeated in his 2008 presidential race but was appointed vice president by Barack Obama. In 2020, he won the presidential election. He was inaugurated into office as the 46th president of the United States of America on January 20, 2021. He is known as "Joe Biden."

Interviewer from Happy Science[*]

Shio Okawa
   Aide to Master & CEO

The Background That Led to This Spiritual Message

In the middle of the night on January 13, 2021, a week prior to Mr. Biden's presidential inaugural ceremony, his guardian spirit came to Master Ryuho Okawa as the original song recording of Master Okawa singing, "Superman Sleeps Too," was playing in the background. This is a lullaby song for which Master Okawa wrote the words and music for the Angel Shoja of Happy Science.

---

[*] Her professional title represents her position at the time of the interview.

1

The Guardian Spirit of Mr. Biden Suddenly Appeared at Night

He appeared to be in pain and revealed who he is

[*Editor's Note—Playing in the background is the original song recording of Master Ryuho Okawa himself singing, "Superman Sleeps Too." Master Ryuho Okawa wrote the words and music to this song as a lullaby for the Angel Shoja of Happy Science.*]

RYUHO OKAWA
It's just as I'd thought. Something's here, even though playing Bach couldn't draw it out.

SHIO OKAWA
That's true.

RYUHO OKAWA
That's incredible. The lullaby can draw it out.

Inside the Mind of President Biden a Week Before the Inauguration

SHIO OKAWA
The lullaby for Angel Shoja is incredible.

RYUHO OKAWA
Incredible.

SHIO OKAWA
Tell me who you are.

BIDEN'S GUARDIAN SPIRIT
Uuuuuuuum … uum … aaah …

SHIO OKAWA
Who's here?

BIDEN'S G.S.
Aaaah … uum. Aaaah. Ha, haa, haa. Aaaah … uum. Ah, ha, ah … [*His breathing shows that he's in pain.*]

SHIO OKAWA
Your face shows that you're in pain. Are you feeling pain? What is the cause of your pain?

BIDEN'S G.S.
Um, uum.

SHIO OKAWA
From Japan?

BIDEN'S G.S.
Umm.

SHIO OKAWA
From America?

BIDEN'S G.S.
Aaaah.

SHIO OKAWA
Can you speak Japanese?

BIDEN'S G.S.
Uum. Aaaah.

SHIO OKAWA
Do you desire to protect peace on Earth?

Inside the Mind of President Biden a Week Before the Inauguration

BIDEN'S G.S.
Aah.

SHIO OKAWA
Do you desire to protect it?

BIDEN'S G.S.
Aah. Aah, ah.

SHIO OKAWA
What's your name?

BIDEN'S G.S.
Aah. It's Biden.

SHIO OKAWA
What's wrong?

BIDEN'S G.S.
Yeah. I'm in pain.

SHIO OKAWA
Do you know Happy Science?

BIDEN'S G.S.
Yes, I've come here before.

SHIO OKAWA
You've (Biden's guardian spirit) been here twice before, actually.

BIDEN'S G.S.
I know.

SHIO OKAWA
You're in pain?

BIDEN'S G.S.
I have pain.

SHIO OKAWA
Don't you think that Mr. Trump is in more pain than you are?

BIDEN'S G.S.
No, I also have pain in my chest.

Inside the Mind of President Biden a Week Before the Inauguration

SHIO OKAWA
Aaah. You have pain in your chest?

BIDEN'S G.S.
Yes.

SHIO OKAWA
Why? Is it because people's thoughts or thought-energy are gathering to you?

BIDEN'S G.S.
Uum, it's kind of ...

SHIO OKAWA
Or is it because of your lifespan?

BIDEN'S G.S.
No, voices are saying, "Die, die," to me.

SHIO OKAWA
Voices are telling you, "Die, die"? But, well, I'm sure that Mr. Trump is probably going through that, too.

BIDEN'S G.S.

Well, I guess he could be. But that's him. So that's nothing that I know about.

SHIO OKAWA

Okay.

BIDEN'S G.S.

Do you hate it that much that I'll become the president?

SHIO OKAWA

Well, we haven't said anything in particular about that.

BIDEN'S G.S.

Actually, what's happening right now hasn't happened in the last 150 years. Why am I being... I guess I'm considerably old.

Inside the Mind of President Biden a Week Before the Inauguration

He pleads for Happy Science to give him a spiritual interview

SHIO OKAWA
How is Mr. Biden feeling?

BIDEN'S G.S.
Please record this during the daytime. You should be doing more work, please. No one here wants to work, it seems.

SHIO OKAWA
No, that's not the reason. The inaugural ceremony is …

BIDEN'S G.S.
If we conduct the spiritual interview during the nighttime, it won't turn out to be such a good one.

SHIO OKAWA
Actually, the state of mind of both of them—Mr. Biden and Mr. Trump—and of America, overall, is abnormal right now.

BIDEN'S G.S.
So, then, you should listen to the views of both sides.

SHIO OKAWA

Even if you say that, he needs to complete the inaugural ceremony first.

BIDEN'S G.S.

That's the reason for the heightened tension.

SHIO OKAWA

Right. That's why a spiritual interview under the current circumstances wouldn't do us much good.... Wouldn't it be better to wait after he officially becomes the president?

BIDEN'S G.S.

No, I need to have one as soon as possible since he could get a heart attack at any moment.

SHIO OKAWA

Don't worry. We can hold spiritual interviews regardless of whether that person is alive or not.

BIDEN'S G.S.

That's only if the person being interviewed is capable of comprehending what's happening. I'm not sure if he can.

Inside the Mind of President Biden a Week Before the Inauguration

SHIO OKAWA
So his (level of understanding spiritual things) is at that sort of level after all?

BIDEN'S G.S.
Yes.

SHIO OKAWA
Well, then I think that that could be the reason for your current condition.

BIDEN'S G.S.
Since I've gotten some practice (with spiritual interviews) now, I'm starting to understand things better.

SHIO OKAWA
Are you his guardian spirit?

BIDEN'S G.S.
Yeah.

SHIO OKAWA
What's your name?

Inside the Mind of President Biden

BIDEN'S G.S.
I don't have one.

SHIO OKAWA
Were you in the Old West?

BIDEN'S G.S.
Yeah, I was a police officer.

SHIO OKAWA
I see.

2

Looking Back at the Confusion of the US Presidential Election

He says China doesn't matter to him because it's on the other side of the Earth

SHIO OKAWA

What are you going to do about China?

BIDEN'S G.S.

What am I going to do about it? What do you mean?

SHIO OKAWA

When you become the president.

BIDEN'S G.S.

Even if you ask me what I'll do, I guess whatever happens will happen. If there's something everyone wants me to do, I'll do that.

SHIO OKAWA

Then let me ask you this: what kind of country do you want America to become?

BIDEN'S G.S.

Hmm? Well, America's fallen to pieces like beef after a butcher's show. So I'll need to stitch things back together again, since we're in a terrible mess. I don't want Trump's "mad cow disease" to spread. America needs to become the "united states" again. There's no unity right now.

SHIO OKAWA

In your view, what does America require for it to unite again?

BIDEN'S G.S.

The red states (predominantly Republican states) are revolting. That's what Trump's . . . Trump's "army of assassins" has been doing. He's the kind of person who recently gave a speech to people saying, "Attack Congress." He's that kind of man who should be shot to death.

Inside the Mind of President Biden a Week Before the Inauguration

SHIO OKAWA

That thought in yourself is the same thing, isn't it. That's why that thought is reflecting back to you. Isn't that what's causing your heart to hurt?

BIDEN'S G.S.

Well, that's one reason. But, of course, there'll be at least a little bit of pain. Many people get heart attacks watching the television. But these people aren't counted among the victims. Even though reports say that only about five people have died in incidents, I'm sure that more have died watching about it on television.

SHIO OKAWA

But before that incident happened, the pro-equality demonstrations held by Democratic supporters led to many injuries. But no one from the Democratic Party has criticized those demonstrations, have they?

BIDEN'S G.S.

Hmmmm, well . . .

SHIO OKAWA
Even though they were supposedly demonstrations protesting racism, some protesters turned into rioters, leading to people's deaths.

BIDEN'S G.S.
Well, that's alright.

SHIO OKAWA
That's when Mr. Trump called for the importance of law and order. But people criticized him for that, saying he's being "racist."

BIDEN'S G.S.
Because he himself isn't abiding by the law and order.

SHIO OKAWA
Actually, the deaths and damage that your party's demonstrations have led to was really terrible.

BIDEN'S G.S.
That's not something that can be helped. The mass media share the responsibility for that, you know. As long as they

supported the Democratic Party and gave me the American presidency, they share the responsibility for doing so. That's not something that can be helped. Aren't I right?

SHIO OKAWA
Well, best of luck to you then.

BIDEN'S G.S.
Yes.

SHIO OKAWA
If you value human rights, then I hope you'll also ask China to value human rights.

BIDEN'S G.S.
Well, with China . . . China's on the opposite side of the Earth, you know. So they don't matter to me. They probably don't have the power to attack us anyway.

He believes that Mr. Trump led America to "insanity"

SHIO OKAWA
But the Democrats are now showing a resemblance to the South Koreans (who imprison their presidents after their presidential terms) and are saying, "We want to throw Mr. Trump into prison" or "We don't want him to run for the presidency again."

BIDEN'S G.S.
Well, even I myself want to shoot him dead, so there must be other people wanting to jail him.

SHIO OKAWA
But, at that rate, America will stop being America.

BIDEN'S G.S.
Well, there's nothing wrong about that in the days of the gunmen. Sheriffs are allowed to shoot down people as much as they want to.

Inside the Mind of President Biden a Week Before the Inauguration

SHIO OKAWA

Well, contradictory to the Democrats' own cries for democracy, their emotions have been driving a lot of their actions.

BIDEN'S G.S.

You're allowed to kill people as long as you have a badge.

SHIO OKAWA

People claim that Mr. Trump is inciting people to riot. But when I look at the mental condition of the Democrats, including Nancy Pelosi, it seems they must have gone mentally insane.

BIDEN'S G.S.

Well, I'm sure that if Trump owned a gun, he would probably also gun down Pelosi and other people.

SHIO OKAWA

Well, I don't know. Look at how he's conducted meetings with someone even like Kim Jong Un.

BIDEN'S G.S.

Hmmm, something like that.... He's the culprit who has driven America to "insanity."

SHIO OKAWA

No, America was already in a state of "insanity." Various issues, including LGBT . . .

BIDEN'S G.S.

LGBT cabinet members . . . the candidates will act.

He appeared today to seek a fair interview to voice his views

SHIO OKAWA

Mr. Biden [*referring to his guardian spirit*], what's your purpose for coming here?

BIDEN'S G.S.

Hmm? Even if you ask me why I came here . . . well, what's proper is . . . well, because I want you to interview me in a fair manner on my views about Trump's riots.

SHIO OKAWA

Well, many channels like CNN and others (who support the Democrats) are already reporting on your views, anyway.

Inside the Mind of President Biden a Week Before the Inauguration

BIDEN'S G.S.

Well, that's . . . I heard that there's a fanatical, delusional religion in Japan, so I need to suppress it from the roots.

SHIO OKAWA

Because *The New York Times* is also . . . Yesterday, we watched the movie, *Mr. Jones*, that depicts the New York Times reporter who concealed the mass massacres committed by the Soviet Union.

BIDEN'S G.S.

Well, that was because . . .

SHIO OKAWA

The movie was saying that *The New York Times* does indeed report fake news.

BIDEN'S G.S.

That's well . . . it can't be helped since *The New York Times* is pro-Soviet. In other words, it's basically a leftist newspaper. That newspaper is friends with the Soviets after all.

SHIO OKAWA

What's your understanding of what we do here? Why did you come here?

BIDEN'S G.S.

Hm? Well, I'm not really sure actually. But it's one of the few places that could let my voice be heard.

SHIO OKAWA

Do you mean that in relation to the spirit world?

BIDEN'S G.S.

In America, we're unable to get information about China. So, since Japan is an ally of the US, I came here to find out Japan's views to use as my reference.

SHIO OKAWA

Then, do you somewhat understand that China and Japan are different countries?

BIDEN'S G.S.

Yeah. I understand that they've been different....

Inside the Mind of President Biden a Week Before the Inauguration

SHIO OKAWA

... that's a fact that you're able to understand?

BIDEN'S G.S.

Taiwan and Japan both don't want to become part of China, I think.

SHIO OKAWA

... so you understand that these countries feel that way?

BIDEN'S G.S.

Yeah.

SHIO OKAWA

I see.

Mr. Biden's guardian spirit seeks a spiritual interview before the inauguration

BIDEN'S G.S.

Hey missis. You know, I think we should have this interview during the daytime. I'll be able to appear more intellectually reliable that way.

SHIO OKAWA

But you didn't come here during the daytime, as I remember it.

BIDEN'S G.S.

Actually, I've been around for a while, but no one wants to let me have an interview.

SHIO OKAWA

Well, first, you should make sure that you'll get through the inaugural ceremony.

BIDEN'S G.S.

Wait, you. But you don't want to interview me, right?

Inside the Mind of President Biden a Week Before the Inauguration

SHIO OKAWA
Right.

BIDEN'S G.S.
You'd rather go out to buy a strawberry *daifuku* mochi cake than hold a spiritual interview with Biden, right? That kind of unenthusiastic work ethic is the actual problem.

SHIO OKAWA
No, that's not the reason. On discussing it with Master Okawa, he also felt that since Mr. Biden and Mr. Trump both seem hot-headed and aren't thinking rationally right now, it will be better to hold one after both of you calm down a little bit. He felt that you'll otherwise just express many extreme opinions.

BIDEN'S G.S.
Wait, that kind of fence-sitting isn't a good thing to do. You should do the right thing and try to find out what's really righteous.

SHIO OKAWA
But even if the interview gets published by Happy Science, most of Americans aren't going to read it, right?

BIDEN'S G.S.

If he gives a speech with the Capitol Hill in the background and says, "All of you, march toward Capitol Hill," then that's practically the French Revolution. He's practically saying, "Go, destroy!"

SHIO OKAWA

Like I said just now, if we hold a spiritual interview right now, won't things like that end up being all that you'll talk about?

BIDEN'S G.S.

Yeah. But that is . . .

SHIO OKAWA

Then it wouldn't be any different from watching the regular news.

BIDEN'S G.S.

Here, there is another . . .

SHIO OKAWA

We want to find out what kind of measures Mr. Biden will carry out as the president of the United States. Even if we asked you about that right now, you would only want to say things that are against Trump.

BIDEN'S G.S.
Well, but you guys are the "Google of the spirit world," so you're supposed to treat people fairly.

SHIO OKAWA
What do we need to treat fairly about?

BIDEN'S G.S.
Well, you should be gathering various kinds of opinions.

SHIO OKAWA
But we listened to Mr. Biden's (his guardian spirit's) opinion[1] last summer, right?

BIDEN'S G.S.
That interview weakened the Japanese people's positive expectations of me.

SHIO OKAWA
But that's your own responsibility. That's not our responsibility.

BIDEN'S G.S.
Well, all the interviewers are thinking, "Biden should be taken down," and are sending out cursing thoughts.

His view that Hillary Clinton should have become president before him

SHIO OKAWA
Does Mr. Biden believe in God?

BIDEN'S G.S.
I am a devout Christian, so . . .

SHIO OKAWA
Can you hear Jesus?

BIDEN'S G.S.
Well, that's not possible. That's only possible if you're close to God after all.

Inside the Mind of President Biden a Week Before the Inauguration

SHIO OKAWA
Well, if you're not more careful, the Democrats could likely be heading toward a democracy without God. They want any kind of human rights to be permitted, right?

BIDEN'S G.S.
Weeeeell.

SHIO OKAWA
They don't seem to understand why God created men and women to be different.

BIDEN'S G.S.
Well, anyway...

SHIO OKAWA
It is not right to discriminate but...

BIDEN'S G.S.
Black people and Yellow people...

SHIO OKAWA

Following the same policies as the Obama–Biden administration will allow drugs, LGBT, and anything else to become legal.

BIDEN'S G.S.

Before we do that, we're trying to eliminate discrimination against Black people, Yellow people, and women. Don't you see that?

SHIO OKAWA

I don't think that appointing incompetent people is a necessary part of eliminating female discrimination. That's not true equality.

BIDEN'S G.S.

Well, I think that Hillary should have become the president before me, for those four years prior to me. If she did, a female American president would've emerged.

Inside the Mind of President Biden a Week Before the Inauguration

3

A Look at the Religious Beliefs of Biden's Guardian Spirit

His view that you can win by siding with what's "scientific"

SHIO OKAWA
Well, I don't necessarily think that Mr. Biden is a bad person.

BIDEN'S G.S.
He's a nice person. But Trump can sometimes be crazy.

SHIO OKAWA
But because Mr. Biden criticizes Trump for not being scientific, this shows that Mr. Biden is closer to being a materialist after all.

BIDEN'S G.S.
Well, America has become a country like that now.

SHIO OKAWA

We're saying that it's wrong to sway to an extreme in that kind of direction.

BIDEN'S G.S.

Well, whether that is wrong or not is ...

SHIO OKAWA

Mr. Biden's side's opinions are encouraging such a thing to happen further, right?

BIDEN'S G.S.

Weeell, weeell, weeell ...

SHIO OKAWA

You're probably also going to sympathize with Ms. Greta again anyway.

BIDEN'S G.S.

Yes, I'm going to. But you know ...

SHIO OKAWA

It is, in fact, a strategy to destroy the world.

BIDEN'S G.S.
But look at everyone—they're all supporting Greta, including Japan, aren't they?

SHIO OKAWA
Then, what is your own view regarding that issue?

BIDEN'S G.S.
Well, I don't know. I don't know. But I can win by siding with what's "scientific."

SHIO OKAWA
That ambiguity of yours is exactly what you need to do something about . . .

He compares Mr. Trump with the jealous god of ancient Israel

BIDEN'S G.S.
Okay, so what I mean is that Trump is trying to embrace the right-wing churches as well as Judaism. I feel that something

about him resembles Jehovah. Maybe that's actually who he is. That jealous god of ancient Israel must be a lot like him.

SHIO OKAWA
I heard that even the prime minister of Israel deleted Trump's photos (from his Twitter account) and people believe that he's trying to distance himself from Trump.

BIDEN'S G.S.
... in spite of how fondly Trump was treating him.

SHIO OKAWA
The prime minister must be the type of man who returns kindness with spite: I couldn't help but feel that way a little bit.

BIDEN'S G.S.
It makes you wonder, doesn't it? After all the things that Trump did for Israel...

In fact, Trump's personality often tends to put personal relationships first. It must come from his business background. That aspect of him is a little...

Inside the Mind of President Biden a Week Before the Inauguration

SHIO OKAWA
But he has more religious faith than you do, don't you think?

BIDEN'S G.S.
No, no.

SHIO OKAWA
In addition to that, the views he has on both global warming and economic policies are closer to the views of God.

BIDEN'S G.S.
No, well, that just means that he's more susceptible to blind faith and fanatical belief than I am.

He's trying to purchase masks from China to foster a closer relationship with Beijing

SHIO OKAWA
The Democratic Party will raise people's taxes again, leading to a huge recession in America, you know.

BIDEN'S G.S.

Well, that . . . well, that is . . .

SHIO OKAWA

Do you understand that?

BIDEN'S G.S.

You should talk about that only if it actually comes.

SHIO OKAWA

What are you referring to by saying, "if it actually comes"? Do you mean the economic depression?

BIDEN'S G.S.

Trump was trying to establish isolationism in America, but I'm trying to reconnect America with the rest of the world. Yeah. I'm going to bring back free trade to America. I'm trying to establish a system of national wealth, you know.

SHIO OKAWA

A system of national wealth? But . . . that's different from establishing free trade.

Inside the Mind of President Biden a Week Before the Inauguration

BIDEN'S G.S.
No, free trade is what it's basically based on.

SHIO OKAWA
It does include free trade. But there was a strong bias in "free trade" that Mr. Trump made efforts to correct. America has no obligation to give the current China any kind of special treatment or any kind of handicap, don't you think so?

BIDEN'S G.S.
Well, there are no more American people who are capable of creating masks, but there are many Chinese people who are.

SHIO OKAWA
That's not a problem because Chinese masks have a terrible reputation around the world. Countries have sent back masks from China, demanding them to be remanufactured.

BIDEN'S G.S.
But the Chinese can make profits if we purchase masks from them, and in this way, they'll purchase American products from us.

SHIO OKAWA
Is your heart feeling better now?

BIDEN'S G.S.
Yes. We have to be friends with China.

He thinks that Happy Science is a New Age movement

SHIO OKAWA
Do you know who Ryuho Okawa is?

BIDEN'S G.S.
Who?

SHIO OKAWA
Do you know Ryuho Okawa?

BIDEN'S G.S.
Well, from coming all the way over here, I know just a little bit about him.

Inside the Mind of President Biden a Week Before the Inauguration

SHIO OKAWA
What do you know about him?

BIDEN'S G.S.
Weeeeell . . .

SHIO OKAWA
But Biden, who's living in the earthly world, doesn't know much, right?

BIDEN'S G.S.
Well . . . if you ask me for my impression of him, I'd say he must be someone similar to Shirley MacLaine.

SHIO OKAWA
I see. Well, that's not necessarily far from what he's like, but . . .

BIDEN'S G.S.
Isn't he doing some kind of a New Age movement?

SHIO OKAWA
Hmmm, how do I say this . . . that's far from what he does. At the same time, it's not extremely wrong either . . .

BIDEN'S G.S.

Well, that's the kind of image I have.

SHIO OKAWA

Well, it's quite far from that actually. He (Master Ryuho Okawa) is God.

BIDEN'S G.S.

No, that's wrong. New Age movements are characterized by channeling practices. And because of these practices, they're not supposed to grow very large. New Age organizations in America aren't supposed to grow larger than 1,000 people. I heard that you (Happy Science) claim to be large though.

SHIO OKAWA

It surely will be nice to get to a point where a spiritual interview with Mr. Biden (his guardian spirit) will invite more Americans to listen to us.

BIDEN'S G.S.

Well, that might possibly happen if the interview is held during the daytime, when my mind's slightly sharper and you get me interviewers who favor me more.

SHIO OKAWA

Doing that won't make any difference, I think. I don't think that's going to happen.

BIDEN'S G.S.

You guys wouldn't get hired by CNN, you know.

SHIO OKAWA

Materialism has already entered America now. I first want to say that the word "scientific" shouldn't be so easily used. You should indicate what the basis for the word "scientific" is.

BIDEN'S G.S.

It's just that there's no benefit gained by being called "unscientific" by others right now.

SHIO OKAWA

It's dangerous to hop on Greta's bandwagon too much, you know. NHK[2] has done this; the carbon emissions segment for its television program was based on news reports claiming drought conditions and lack of snowfall. But the television program turned out to be very wrong about that—look at the huge snowstorms that are sweeping the world right now and leading to people suffering.

BIDEN'S G.S.
Hmmmm. So, the issue about what Japan's going to do about its energy resources—that's up to Japan's own national measures. That should be something Japan itself should think about. I guess solar panels aren't going to be useful in snowy weather conditions.

He speaks about his past-life relationship with Barack Obama

SHIO OKAWA
Do you pray to God when you're not sure about something?

BIDEN'S G.S.
Well, I do go to church on occasion, of course. But because of the coronavirus, it's better not to go to church right now.

Inside the Mind of President Biden a Week Before the Inauguration

SHIO OKAWA
Is your guiding spirit Mr. Obama, then?

BIDEN'S G.S.
What? What do you mean?

SHIO OKAWA
Because you've mentioned him so frequently.

BIDEN'S G.S.
Well, that's because we used to work together in the previous administration.

SHIO OKAWA
Isn't that the reason Mr. Obama is backing you up?

BIDEN'S G.S.
Well, that's because Mr. Obama is the chieftain of the Dogon tribe, of course.

SHIO OKAWA
There's a bit of evil in Mr. Obama though.

BIDEN'S G.S.
Obama is . . . Obama is the "chieftain," so he's a "religious leader." Him, too.

SHIO OKAWA
If you get to a position like America's president, I'm sure that someone will become your guiding spirit.

BIDEN'S G.S.
Well, so, he was sent to America for the purpose of bringing it to destruction.

SHIO OKAWA
Mr. Obama was sent?

BIDEN'S G.S.
Yeah.

SHIO OKAWA
Sent by who?

Inside the Mind of President Biden a Week Before the Inauguration

BIDEN'S G.S.
Hm? Well, he became America's president to make the country collectively repent for forcefully bringing African slaves to America 400 years ago.

SHIO OKAWA
Oh, the purpose was to make America reap that karma?

BIDEN'S G.S.
Yeah, yeah, yeah. And his job is to crush the White people.

SHIO OKAWA
Is that so.

BIDEN'S G.S.
That's why Mr. Trump deserves to be beaten right now.

SHIO OKAWA
But you told us (in the previous spiritual interview) that you were the one who brought (Mr. Obama's) ancestors to America.

BIDEN'S G.S.
Oh, that might be true.

SHIO OKAWA

You're the one who should actually be reaping that karma. So why is he giving you his support?

BIDEN'S G.S.

Hm? I'm not really sure. But he made me his vice president, you know.

SHIO OKAWA

Oh, I see.

BIDEN'S G.S.

Uuuum, because he thought that someone of senior age has wisdom.

Biden's guiding spirit will probably be similar to Jimmy Carter's guiding spirit

BIDEN'S G.S.

Anyway, it can't be helped. Mr. Trump was ... But I'm sure that supporting him will be of no worth to you because he

Inside the Mind of President Biden a Week Before the Inauguration

will only invite people to dislike himself, you know. It can't be helped, you see.

He's popular with just a group of people—the fanatics—but other sensible people think that he's dangerous.

SHIO OKAWA
No. They're not just "a group of people" though, right? Just look at how the votes were basically nearly 50–50.

BIDEN'S G.S.
Hmmm.

SHIO OKAWA
So they're not just "a part of" the people, don't you think so? The votes show that a considerable number of them support him.

BIDEN'S G.S.
Well, the radicals want to be able to destroy the Democratic Party so they want to start a "Civil War."

SHIO OKAWA

Then, will that be enough? We should hold the spiritual interview after the inaugural ceremony is safely over and you're officially the president of the United States.

BIDEN'S G.S.

It's still the daytime in America right now. Yeah.

SHIO OKAWA

If that's the case, you should get back to your work.

BIDEN'S G.S.

Weeell...

SHIO OKAWA

Is there going to be a guiding spirit?

BIDEN'S G.S.

Well, since you won't let me have a two-hour (spiritual interview), we need to record these bit-by-bit to get enough content to publish a book.

SHIO OKAWA

You've even thought that part through [*laughs wryly*].

Inside the Mind of President Biden a Week Before the Inauguration

BIDEN'S G.S.
Hmmm.

SHIO OKAWA
Is there going to be a guiding spirit?

BIDEN'S G.S.
Hm?

SHIO OKAWA
A guiding spirit. Are there plans for there to be one?

BIDEN'S G.S.
Hmmm. Well, there will probably be one similar to former President Jimmy Carter's.

SHIO OKAWA
Hm? Aaah, I see. You know, people have been saying that you're going to be as weak a president as Jimmy Carter was.

BIDEN'S G.S.
Well, I'm pretty sure that I'll only serve one term. Probably.

SHIO OKAWA

. . . You yourself think so, too.

BIDEN'S G.S.

Yeah. So, the next president will be a black female.

Inside the Mind of President Biden a Week Before the Inauguration

4

How Does President Biden Plan to Deal with the Coronavirus Crisis?

Biden wants to deport Trump from the country

SHIO OKAWA
Then, is there something that Mr. Biden wants to accomplish the most—is there some keyword?

BIDEN'S G.S.
Hmm...

SHIO OKAWA
Even if he only serves for one term, does he have something, some kind of work, that he at the very least desires to leave behind?

BIDEN'S G.S.
That would be to deport Trump from the country.

SHIO OKAWA
No, no. I mean as a job.

BIDEN'S G.S.
Isn't that a job?

SHIO OKAWA
No, I'm asking you in terms of America's national policy or some kind of general principle that you want to lay out.

BIDEN'S G.S.
So, I want to transfer Trump to Israel and get him to become a naturalized citizen of Israel.

SHIO OKAWA
Why do you hate him so much anyway?

BIDEN'S G.S.
I can't stand being in the same country as him.

SHIO OKAWA
Well [*smiles wryly*], so, since you've almost solely criticized Mr. Trump in the election campaign rather than talk about your own policies, people are saying that they have no idea what you're going to do.

Inside the Mind of President Biden a Week Before the Inauguration

BIDEN'S G.S.

Since my votes outnumbered his votes, just be quiet and congratulate me. Yeah. There's no need to put me to shame, don't you think?

SHIO OKAWA

The American mass media, such as CNN, has really shown the shameful side of itself this time. We saw how much the actions of people inside that kind of mass media channel are based on their own subjective views.

BIDEN'S G.S.

Well, when Trump got elected, even Obama and Hillary congratulated him, you know. It's important to be polite.

SHIO OKAWA

Then, if Mr. Trump had done that, would you have not wanted to deport him?

BIDEN'S G.S.

Hm, well, I would've let him off by just sending him to jail for his scandal with the Kremlin, or something like that.

SHIO OKAWA

See, he reacted that way because of this kind of hidden intention inside yourself, don't you see that?

BIDEN'S G.S.

Hmm...

SHIO OKAWA

It's because he can tell that you want to arrest him.

BIDEN'S G.S.

Yeah. Otherwise, if he'd gotten elected, he'd have arrested me for my scandal with Beijing.

SHIO OKAWA

But haven't you also actually sent e-mails (to Beijing), right?

BIDEN'S G.S.

Well, it's not like there hadn't been a scandal with Russia, either.

SHIO OKAWA

But there isn't a Devil particularly possessing the Kremlin right now. But there is, indeed, a Devil possessing Beijing.

Inside the Mind of President Biden a Week Before the Inauguration

BIDEN'S G.S.

Well, so, since I'll have to fight both Beijing and the Kremlin, I'll just pretend to apply pressure on Beijing but attack Russia.

Why Biden doesn't want to investigate whether Beijing's scheme is behind the coronavirus crisis

SHIO OKAWA

Do you really believe that Beijing was not the source of the coronavirus crisis?

BIDEN'S G.S.

I've never even considered that idea.

SHIO OKAWA

Why haven't you?

BIDEN'S G.S.

There is no way that, hmmm, they would do such a thing.

SHIO OKAWA
Why wouldn't they?

BIDEN'S G.S.
It's unthinkable. We are their biggest trading partner. There's no way that they would do that.

SHIO OKAWA
But Beijing wants to rule the world.

BIDEN'S G.S.
I've no knowledge of that.

SHIO OKAWA
That's why Beijing wants to destroy America, you know.

BIDEN'S G.S.
America was already ruling the world.

SHIO OKAWA
No, so . . . you're really behind the times, aren't you?

Inside the Mind of President Biden a Week Before the Inauguration

BIDEN'S G.S.

Well, so Trump wants to imagine things like that. That's why he's saying, "America first . . .," so he won't be defeated by China.

SHIO OKAWA

With so many of your own people dying, wouldn't you normally want to figure out what caused the coronavirus?

BIDEN'S G.S.

If we investigate and find out that it was a scheme plotted by Beijing, there will be a nuclear war, you know? That's why it would be better not to find out such an answer.

SHIO OKAWA

Wait. In that case, are you okay that at this rate, only your own people are going to continue dying? Because of the virus variants that are appearing, it's possible that the vaccines won't be so effective.

BIDEN'S G.S.

Hmm, but that happening would be better than a nuclear war erupting.

SHIO OKAWA

I'm not recommending a nuclear war to start, but Beijing will probably continue its various schemes again.

BIDEN'S G.S.

Well, if we end up in a nuclear war, then there will be tens of millions of deaths. Really . . .

SHIO OKAWA

Nothing is wrong with avoiding that. But unless you give the coronavirus crisis a proper investigation right now, Beijing will continue to commit much greater evils (than even now).

BIDEN'S G.S.

That's the reason why it's important to look the other way if it's only going to result in an even greater tragedy.

SHIO OKAWA

Alright. Well, it's true that that way of thinking is also deeply rooted in Japan.

BIDEN'S G.S.

Hmm. So, anyway, if we resume our former trading relationship with China, I think that Beijing will stop doing things like this. And it's clear that with such a scheme as the coronavirus, it will travel around the world in the end, making it impossible for Beijing to develop friendly relations with any country. The coronavirus is going to spread to its own country in the end, so it's not possible for them to win a one-sided victory.

He says that Biden will press the missile-launch button if everyone tells him to

SHIO OKAWA
Mr. Obama said that Mr. Hatoyama[3] was the most difficult Japanese prime minister to get along with.

BIDEN'S G.S.
They are similar types of people.

SHIO OKAWA
Oh, Mr. Obama and Mr. Hatoyama are?

BIDEN'S G.S.
Yeah.

SHIO OKAWA
Oh, are they?

BIDEN'S G.S.
Well, they're both utopian socialists, which makes them similar.

SHIO OKAWA
Are you saying that they're idealists?

BIDEN'S G.S.
Yeah. They're both similar in that way.

SHIO OKAWA
What about Mr. Biden and Mr. Hatoyama?

BIDEN'S G.S.
Well, I don't know much about Mr. Hatoyama, actually . . .

SHIO OKAWA
But Mr. Obama had pressed a missile-launch button during his presidency, you know.

Inside the Mind of President Biden a Week Before the Inauguration

BIDEN'S G.S.
He pressed it?

SHIO OKAWA
Not a nuclear one ...

BIDEN'S G.S.
Oh, you're saying that he shot a missile.

SHIO OKAWA
He launched pinpoint missile attacks, right?

BIDEN'S G.S.
Yeah, yeah, yeah. That's right; he did. He might have done that.

SHIO OKAWA
So, I think that Mr. Obama was stronger than Mr. Hatoyama ...

BIDEN'S G.S.
Isn't Mr. Hatoyama someone of the past?

SHIO OKAWA
Yes, he's in the past.

BIDEN'S G.S.
Yeah. Well, I'll press the button if everyone tells me to.

Why Biden's guardian spirit can speak Japanese

SHIO OKAWA
It seems that (your way of thinking) is close to Japanese people's way of thinking. Perhaps you've been born in Japan before.

BIDEN'S G.S.
Hmmm?

SHIO OKAWA
You even speak Japanese fluently.

BIDEN'S G.S.
Japan . . . No, well, since I'm Christian, I don't acknowledge reincarnations like that.

Inside the Mind of President Biden a Week Before the Inauguration

SHIO OKAWA
You don't seem to be someone of really high spiritual grade, but you don't seem to be a very evil Devil either. So I feel that you must be somewhere in heaven. And, since you're able to speak Japanese so fluently, this must mean that . . .

BIDEN'S G.S.
Well, I've visited here several times and there was someone who taught me.

SHIO OKAWA
Someone is teaching you?

BIDEN'S G.S.
Hmm . . . I'm really not sure, but there seem to also be bilinguals in Japan.

SHIO OKAWA
Aah.

BIDEN'S G.S.
Someone like them immediately dubs my words for me.

SHIO OKAWA
Is that so.

BIDEN'S G.S.
Yeah. Since I couldn't speak it at first.

SHIO OKAWA
Is that right. I see.

BIDEN'S G.S.
Hmmm. Hasn't Mr. Trump (his guardian spirit) recently been speaking Japanese, too?

SHIO OKAWA
But he kept speaking only in English in the beginning.

BIDEN'S G.S.
Yeah. Aah . . . [*sighs*].

Inside the Mind of President Biden a Week Before the Inauguration

What will he do if he can't stop the coronavirus' spread after succeeding Trump?

SHIO OKAWA
Do you see Iran as an evil country?

BIDEN'S G.S.
I don't really know.

SHIO OKAWA
I see.

BIDEN'S G.S.
I'm wondering what to do. Compared with the requests during Trump's presidency, they'll make more requests to me to lift their sanctions. So...

SHIO OKAWA
So, you're going to ease their sanctions a little?

BIDEN'S G.S.
Well, personality-wise, I tend to believe in not ruffling too many of the world's feathers.

SHIO OKAWA
Alright. I see.

BIDEN'S G.S.
Well, he (Mr. Trump) likes to fight, you know. The American people have had enough of him. So it can't be helped.

SHIO OKAWA
The coronavirus crisis was a huge (reason for that) though, you know.

BIDEN'S G.S.
Well, yeah, the coronavirus crisis was. But it's true that he's also extreme.

SHIO OKAWA
I'd advise you to be careful. In Japan, Mr. Abe resigned because of it. But even after Mr. Suga took office, the conditions haven't improved at all, after all.

BIDEN'S G.S.
Yeah.

Inside the Mind of President Biden a Week Before the Inauguration

SHIO OKAWA

It's been causing his approval ratings to drop. So I think that the spread of the coronavirus probably won't weaken just by your taking office.

BIDEN'S G.S.

Yeah. If masks and vaccines aren't able to prevent it, I do think that my approval ratings will probably gradually drop.

SHIO OKAWA

Right. So that's a serious matter.

BIDEN'S G.S.

Hmm... Well, it can't be helped. It's a problem that a country that's supposed to be saving others is suffering the most damage.

SHIO OKAWA

That fact should be raising a suspicion in you, don't you think so?

He wants to keep the US–Beijing joint research on the coronavirus from getting exposed

BIDEN'S G.S.

Hmmm. Well, things could get bad if we too deeply investigate the coronavirus issue. Actually, the coronavirus was a joint research conducted by America and Beijing.

SHIO OKAWA

Until part-way through it, right?

BIDEN'S G.S.

Yeah. America realized that it's dangerous and pulled out of it. But Beijing decided to continue. And as we had expected, the result is this.

SHIO OKAWA

I see. So you're saying that that is the reason America can't investigate it?

BIDEN'S G.S.

America pulled out of it part way along.

SHIO OKAWA
Well, then, wouldn't things be fine, since America withdrew?

BIDEN'S G.S.
But we don't want to reveal that to the world. That's why we are silent.

SHIO OKAWA
I see. You're saying that your country will suffer damage if the truth is revealed?

BIDEN'S G.S.
When America says that the research started 15 years ago, this means that our joint research with Beijing started. But in the middle of it, America realized the danger of it and withdrew. But Beijing continued the research and finally conducted experimental tests.

SHIO OKAWA
Well, if that is something that Mr. Biden also knows deeply about, then . . .

BIDEN'S G.S.

He knows about that but America also wouldn't want something like that to get discovered.

SHIO OKAWA

I see.

BIDEN'S G.S.

If they say, "You're an accomplice, too," that would be the end of things. It will stop there. If they say that Americans killed Americans, the responsibility will . . . The American scientist's name will be discovered anyway. So it's the same either way.

SHIO OKAWA

I see.

BIDEN'S G.S.

America is also responsible for it, so we can't blame everything on Beijing since we were conducting the research together. It's something that we realize. Yeah. We actually withdrew though; we said that we can't research something this dangerous anymore and pulled out.

Inside the Mind of President Biden a Week Before the Inauguration

SHIO OKAWA

You mean that it will damage America's honor?

BIDEN'S G.S.

Yeah. I don't want it to get exposed. Some fields can be researched jointly. But there are certain fields that shouldn't be. For example, weapons development is one area that shouldn't be.

5

Looking Into the Character of Mr. Biden, the President-Elect

The way he views China's surveillance society and the crisis in Hong Kong

SHIO OKAWA

But, regardless, I still want to believe that Mr. Biden and Nancy Pelosi will insist on protecting human rights. So, when Mr. Biden becomes the president, I hope that he won't forget the world's numerous people who are suffering suppression under Beijing's rule.

BIDEN'S G.S.

Well, when it comes to killing someone, even Trump is faint-hearted. Even he hasn't done much of that. He's only done it a little bit. Even as the president, he's only done small things like target individual people.

SHIO OKAWA

But I really pray that you will make democracy under God flourish.

Inside the Mind of President Biden a Week Before the Inauguration

BIDEN'S G.S.
Well, it's fine that he believes in God. But he needs better refinement. At the current rate, he's just a roughneck in people's eyes, you know.

SHIO OKAWA
But your son might be receiving large sums of money from China.

BIDEN'S G.S.
Well, receiving money from others is a good thing to do.

SHIO OKAWA
Pardon me?

BIDEN'S G.S.
Although *giving* money isn't such a good thing to do.

SHIO OKAWA
With that kind of thinking, the self-help thinking that led America to prosperity will vanish.

BIDEN'S G.S.

Weeell, I mean, when I say "receiving money," I mean that China has money reserves. It has a lot of accumulated foreign currency reserves, you know. He was able to get China to invest those reserves in America by telling them that we'll use that money for them, that's all. That was a good thing that he did.

SHIO OKAWA

So you're saying you extracted some of China's financial reserves.

BIDEN'S G.S.

For the interests of America. Since China was accumulating more and more foreign currency reserves, it's good to encourage China to invest in America rather than in some other bad thing. Anyway, I don't think that what he's done is as bad as people have said it is. So, well, I have a milder personality than him (Mr. Trump). Yeah.

SHIO OKAWA

Well, I hope that you won't behave overly mild . . . And there's also the fact that China's surveillance society has already made huge progress.

Inside the Mind of President Biden a Week Before the Inauguration

BIDEN'S G.S.

Well, it doesn't really matter if Chinese people are keeping other Chinese people under heavy surveillance.

SHIO OKAWA

Actually, Beijing's web of fingers is stretching out to other areas of the world like America and Europe.

BIDEN'S G.S.

Well, if that's the case, the Chinese people should revolt. And, well, it can't be helped if the people aren't able to do so, don't you think?

SHIO OKAWA

But even if they try to protest, they'll be thrown into prison and get killed.

BIDEN'S G.S.

Well, that can't be helped, then. (Beijing) does things like that because it thinks that there will be bigger gains by doing so, aren't I right?

SHIO OKAWA
When Mr. Biden became (the president-elect), more than 50 people in Hong Kong got arrested immediately.

BIDEN'S G.S.
That's probably because Beijing intends to incorporate Hong Kong into China. It's as clear as day that only the Communist Party is in their future prospects.

SHIO OKAWA
I'm guessing you're saying that you've given up on (helping) the crisis there.

BIDEN'S G.S.
It's clear that we can only abandon that issue. In return, Beijing will have lost the third top financial city of the world.

Inside the Mind of President Biden a Week Before the Inauguration

He believes the mass media hates Trump because he "responds by badmouthing about them"

SHIO OKAWA
Okay. I think you're right now about the same as the Roman Catholic pope.

BIDEN'S G.S.
I don't really understand what you mean by that.

SHIO OKAWA
It's okay. The people who watch this interview (and the one with the pope's guardian spirit[4]) will understand what I'm saying.

BIDEN'S G.S.
I'm sure that the pope himself is an important person. But I don't really understand what you're saying.

SHIO OKAWA
He says that he cannot hear the voice of Jesus.

BIDEN'S G.S.
That's probably because Jesus is such a great figure.

SHIO OKAWA

Actually, right now you're in the body of the one whom Jesus called Heavenly Father.

BIDEN'S G.S.

Is that so? Well, I don't think any American would believe you.

SHIO OKAWA

Well, America probably has to learn something of another level, too.

BIDEN'S G.S.

Even if Mr. Trump calls the name of God, everyone—the mass media—is suspicious of his honesty. They believe that he could be only trying to rationalize his actions.

SHIO OKAWA

No. People in the mass media and the politicians have never been business executives like Mr. Trump has, which is why they can't comprehend the meaning of his actions.

BIDEN'S G.S.

Well, but how do I say this—but still he should try harder to gain people's understanding. It's fine to be a business executive, I guess. But a business executive normally can't succeed by being disliked by others.

SHIO OKAWA
Wait. As I've been saying, since more than 70 million people have voted for him, it's not that he's disliked by people. Don't you see that?

BIDEN'S G.S.
Hmm...

SHIO OKAWA
It's only the Democrats and the mass media who have fierce hatred toward him. Other than that, it's just some people in Hollywood and leftist groups.

BIDEN'S G.S.
The mass media hates (Trump) because he responds by bad-mouthing about them, right?

SHIO OKAWA
Yeah, okay.

BIDEN'S G.S.

But politicians in Japan aren't able to criticize the mass media, right? Probably.

SHIO OKAWA

Yes.

BIDEN'S G.S.

Japanese politicians just endure fierce one-sided criticism, right? And then they'll resign if something is written about them because the mass media criticizes them too much. Isn't that what happens in Japan? But it's true that the mass media's business will go under unless they sell enough of their news.

SHIO OKAWA

Well, it's not such an easy world to live in these days.

Inside the Mind of President Biden a Week Before the Inauguration

Said in a "positive" way, Biden is someone favorable to Japanese people's tastes

BIDEN'S G.S.

Well, this is the type of person that I am. But if you look at me in a positive light, I might at least be someone favorable to Japanese people's tastes.

SHIO OKAWA

Yes, I agree with you. Your way of thinking is similar to the Japanese people's mindset. So you might become popular among the Japanese people.

BIDEN'S G.S.

I think so, too. Also, America's feelings are on edge right now, so I'm trying to make it a little more moderate as a country.

SHIO OKAWA

You want to ease things, right?

BIDEN'S G.S.

Doing so is one of my roles, I think. If Trump had plunged into things, there really could have been a thermonuclear war. But since I . . . well I might lack the ability . . . but I think it's fine if people feel grateful for my efforts in developing a better friendship with Beijing.

SHIO OKAWA
But in the end, many people will end up dying due to the coronavirus.

BIDEN'S G.S.
We've developed a vaccine for that, so things will work out somehow.

SHIO OKAWA
Haven't there been more American deaths due to the coronavirus than due to the war?

BIDEN'S G.S.
That's true with regard to the death tolls in America. But the global death tolls of World War I and World War II were very high.

Inside the Mind of President Biden a Week Before the Inauguration

He says Trump is a "magician" who enchants people

SHIO OKAWA
Regarding Trump's supporters who went to the Capitol building...

BIDEN'S G.S.
About that... Trump needs to have better sportsmanship. He should come to Japan to learn the bushido spirit.

SHIO OKAWA
What is Mr. Biden's impression of those people?

BIDEN'S G.S.
Who do you mean?

SHIO OKAWA
The Trump supporters. If you want to ease things, wouldn't you also need to persuade his supporters?

BIDEN'S G.S.
Well, I haven't said that Trump doesn't have any ability. I think that Trump must be a wizard after all. He's a type

of magician who can enchant people. He has the ability to enchant people. I think so. It's that mind of fanatic belief or blind faith. So you could say he is more suited to being the head of a religion. That's the kind of ability he has. He can lead people with strong words.

SHIO OKAWA
Isn't Mr. Obama also a little like that type of person? Or I should rather say that Mr. Obama's speech writer was like that. The speech writer was impressive.

BIDEN'S G.S.
Obama was aiming to be the modern Jesus.

SHIO OKAWA
It's not possible for him to be.

BIDEN'S G.S.
He thought that his words were words that Jesus would have said. But Obama did indeed seem weak in terms of this world. Well, the two-party system in America helps maintain balance by alternating between the two parties.

Inside the Mind of President Biden a Week Before the Inauguration

SHIO OKAWA
I see.

BIDEN'S G.S.
So if I don't do a good job, then the administration might switch to the others (the Republicans). But I don't know if Mr. Trump will be able to stay angry during these coming four years. I think that Nancy Pelosi is trying to wrap him in chains so that he won't be able to run for president again.

SHIO OKAWA
She's ensuring that he will never be able to make a comeback, isn't she? But something doesn't feel right about going as far as she is.

BIDEN'S G.S.
They're both rude to each other, so it can't be helped.

SHIO OKAWA
They're both behaving that way.

To acquire the market of 1.4 billion Chinese people he wants to avoid ruining relations with Beijing

SHIO OKAWA

I hope Mr. Biden will have a safe inaugural ceremony then...

BIDEN'S G.S.

Well, I'm not so intelligent, but as a White American, I'm at least a member of the establishment (the class with an established social authority). So it's not that...

SHIO OKAWA

Well, you're probably a "nice" person.

BIDEN'S G.S.

At the same time, I've opened my heart to Black people, Asians, and women.

SHIO OKAWA

That's a good thing, sure.

Inside the Mind of President Biden a Week Before the Inauguration

BIDEN'S G.S.

So people will see less of the good points that were in Mr. Trump. But there will also be less of the bad aspects of Mr. Trump. America will become easier to talk to.

SHIO OKAWA

But Mr. Trump isn't a racist person.

BIDEN'S G.S.

But when he gets into a fight . . .

SHIO OKAWA

That's the image of him that the mass media intentionally created.

BIDEN'S G.S.

No, it wasn't just the mass media, you know. He often said that he'll raise trade tariffs to 200 percent.

SHIO OKAWA

But before the coronavirus crisis, America's economy was doing very well, don't you remember? Even the unemployment rate had gone down.

BIDEN'S G.S.
No one acknowledges him for that though.

SHIO OKAWA
That's because the coronavirus appeared, leading people to forget that he accomplished that. Also, he treats Black people in the same way he treats others.

BIDEN'S G.S.
No, you see, that's not right. In America, Mr. Obama is thought to have overcome the great depression caused by the Republican Party, you know. During those eight years of his term.

SHIO OKAWA
Okay. That was right after the Lehman crisis.

BIDEN'S G.S.
Yeah, he inherited that situation, and he fixed it. He saved the unfortunate people.

SHIO OKAWA
But there was a side of him that destroyed the wealthy class of people, the American Dream.

Inside the Mind of President Biden a Week Before the Inauguration

BIDEN'S G.S.

No, he only crushed to pieces the people who cheated to make financial profits, that's all.

SHIO OKAWA

Your son is part of those people, actually.

BIDEN'S G.S.

Well, it's true that we're not necessarily financially poor, I guess. We're financially wealthy, it's true.

SHIO OKAWA

Well, that's a good thing if it leads to America getting better.

BIDEN'S G.S.

But even though I have money, I own only approximately 600 million yen (approximately 6 million US dollars). On the other hand, Mr. Trump owns more than a trillion yen (10 billion US dollars).

SHIO OKAWA

But Mr. Trump earned that money through his own business.

BIDEN'S G.S.

Yeah, his desires for self-gain or self-interest can influence him.

SHIO OKAWA

No, I'm more suspicious of you and your son with regard to that, even if you're running your own company and operating your own business...

BIDEN'S G.S.

Since Hollywood, California, wants the market of 1.4 billion Chinese people right now, it doesn't want us to get so unfriendly with Beijing.

SHIO OKAWA

I see that Hollywood wants that market. But being hypocritical is a wrong way to be. It's wrong of it to do a lot of "killing" on the movie screens but then to promote a wrong sense of justice in response.

BIDEN'S G.S.

Well, I'm not the only person who's running the government. Other people are running it, too. There's also Congress and judicial courts. Mr. Trump had seemed to forget about the separation of powers and thought that he was doing everything on his own. He was a little bit like that.

6

How Biden's Guardian Spirit Considers the Role of America's President

He imagines the role of America's president as just an honorary one

SHIO OKAWA

Well, if you're going to lead America, then . . .

BIDEN'S G.S.

I'd be glad if I can get another spiritual interview some other time, so I can appear more respectable.

SHIO OKAWA

Okay. I'd still like to wait until after the inaugural ceremony and until you've officially become the American president. That will let us find out more about what will happen from now on.

BIDEN'S G.S.

You guys don't think I'll be alive until January 20, isn't that what you're thinking?

Inside the Mind of President Biden a Week Before the Inauguration

SHIO OKAWA

No, we aren't imagining such a thing. We think that you will be alive.

BIDEN'S G.S.

Hmm? The Trump supporters are trying to kill me in the earthly sense, you know.

SHIO OKAWA

Well, that's a mutual thing between both of you, as far as I can see.

BIDEN'S G.S.

Hmm... Well, that's...

SHIO OKAWA

Involved in that are the mass media, the Democrats and their supporters, Nancy Pelosi, the people of CNN, and the newspapers.

BIDEN'S G.S.

Mr. Trump and his followers are sending cursing prayers to me, hoping for my dementia to suddenly get worse.

SHIO OKAWA

You will have very heavy responsibilities to take care of, so please stay healthy, both mentally and physically, and do the best that you can.

BIDEN'S G.S.

Weeell, I think I'll only be serving one term.

SHIO OKAWA

That's a rather apprehensive outlook . . . [*smiles wryly*].

BIDEN'S G.S.

No, no. Well, it's true that there are wounds Mr. Trump created. That's something I will heal, so forgive me. Well, just think of it as your own father[5] becoming the president. That's what I will be like.

SHIO OKAWA

No, no. That's hard to accept.

BIDEN'S G.S.

That's basically what it's going to be like.

Inside the Mind of President Biden a Week Before the Inauguration

SHIO OKAWA

No, well, I understand that you're a nice person. You're a nice person, yes. But what will happen when a nice person gains power is something that you'll need to put some efforts into.

BIDEN'S G.S.

Well, there are smart people surrounding me, so I'll be alright.

SHIO OKAWA

Are they truly smart people . . .? I'm not so sure about that.

BIDEN'S G.S.

There's a former Fed chair who I've entrusted a little bit of the financial matters to, so she'll take care of them somehow. That area is beyond my understanding anyway.

SHIO OKAWA

You're only going to take an honorary role then.

BIDEN'S G.S.

Yes, of course. It's alright for a president to handle things in that way.

SHIO OKAWA

Pardon me?! No, that's not what America's president should do.

BIDEN'S G.S.

Since I'm the head of state, I only have to sit and act like Queen Elizabeth.

SHIO OKAWA

Oh my goodness! I'm not so sure about that.

BIDEN'S G.S.

That's fine. I'll be wearing a mask, and if that proves to be an effective measure, then that itself will give my becoming the president its meaning.

SHIO OKAWA

It sounds to me that your religious faith is a little weak after all.

BIDEN'S G.S.

Well, Japan seems progressive to me. I think it's very impressive that the coronavirus has spread very little in Japan. I'm just trying to follow what Japan is doing, don't you see that?

Inside the Mind of President Biden a Week Before the Inauguration

SHIO OKAWA

Well, it shouldn't merely be about promoting human rights, about thinking of what science says, or about democracy without God. Please establish a democracy under God . . . Please remember that you will be putting your left hand on the Bible and taking the oath of office during your inaugural ceremony.

BIDEN'S G.S.

Well, I do also believe that human life is more valuable than polar bears' lives.

SHIO OKAWA

We definitely need you to feel that way, even if other people don't.

BIDEN'S G.S.

Mr. Trump's performances had been a bit over-the-top.

He says that it's good for a simpleton to become the president

BIDEN'S G.S.
Wait, what are you doing there? What's that? What are you doing?

SHIO OKAWA
Oh, I'm just getting a little bit sleepy; that's all.

BIDEN'S G.S.
Oh, really? There's not enough grit in you, you know.

SHIO OKAWA
It's already 1:30 (a.m.).

BIDEN'S G.S.
That's because you won't wake up in the morning.

SHIO OKAWA
No. I'm not able to get enough sleep at night due to things like this happening.

Inside the Mind of President Biden a Week Before the Inauguration

BIDEN'S G.S.

You'll have no choice but to work at night then.

SHIO OKAWA

But you came (at this timing) because it's currently the middle of the day in your area.

BIDEN'S G.S.

It's the middle of the day in America right now.

SHIO OKAWA

See?

BIDEN'S G.S.

It will soon be time for my nap.

SHIO OKAWA

You're doing things like this to Master so that . . . On the other hand, you'll return home feeling full of energy, won't you?

BIDEN'S G.S.

Hmm . . .

SHIO OKAWA

Even if you don't get fully energized, you'll still go home feeling a little healed from receiving a shower of light, won't you?

BIDEN'S G.S.

Well, I have to put a lid on the source of the badmouthing that's coming from Japan, you know.

SHIO OKAWA

That's not at all what we're doing. We're not the source of badmouthing.

BIDEN'S G.S.

American presidents often use preemptive strikes.

SHIO OKAWA

Master Okawa also clearly said at Tokyo Shoshinkan (during his lecture entitled, "A Lecture on *The Laws of Secret*") that he's not at all an extreme type of person.

BIDEN'S G.S.

But he doesn't like Biden, right? Anyway, that's fine. It's a good thing for a simpleton to be able to serve as president.

Inside the Mind of President Biden a Week Before the Inauguration

SHIO OKAWA
No, that's hard to believe.

BIDEN'S G.S.
There will be peace on Earth.

SHIO OKAWA
Right now is the worst timing to have a president who is a "simpleton."

BIDEN'S G.S.
Hmmm? But even Xi Jinping is a "simpleton"...

SHIO OKAWA
Well, yes.

BIDEN'S G.S.
He believes that he's smart though. That's why things like that are happening there.

SHIO OKAWA
That's the issue. When you try to do things despite the lack of ability in yourself, this causes evil sometimes.

BIDEN'S G.S.
At least I'm self-aware that I'm a simpleton.

SHIO OKAWA
Oh, I see. You're aware of it.

BIDEN'S G.S.
I'm not smart like Angela Merkel is. I'm aware of that, you know.

SHIO OKAWA
I see.

BIDEN'S G.S.
That's why there will be peace, do you see?

SHIO OKAWA
Okay.

BIDEN'S G.S.
Hmmm. Hmmm. Well, anyway, I'm a gentle lamb.

Inside the Mind of President Biden a Week Before the Inauguration

Will America be able to stop Beijing's evil from now on?

SHIO OKAWA
I really think it's time for both parties (in America) to stop hating each other. It's about time for the Democratic Party to stop behaving that way. It's in such a frenzy that it now resembles South Korea.

BIDEN'S G.S.
Well, you're going to change your mind, you know? Trump (his guardian spirit) will be coming here eventually. When he (his guardian spirit) does and you listen (to what he says), you'll change your mind, you know?

SHIO OKAWA
That's possible.

BIDEN'S G.S.
Yeah. Because things he says are extreme.

SHIO OKAWA
But I believe that what Mr. Trump says also comes from his sense of responsibility. It's possible that Beijing will attack.

BIDEN'S G.S.

Well, I'm not a Buddhist, but I do want to tell Trump this: "You have an attachment." He needs to be told to cut away his attachment more.

SHIO OKAWA

But isn't that also true about yourself?

BIDEN'S G.S.

Since I was elected, I have the right (to become the president) anyway.

SHIO OKAWA

Fine.

BIDEN'S G.S.

I've lost my wife and child before and bounced back from such circumstances of life. There's a side of me that resembles Lincoln.

SHIO OKAWA

In the eyes of people like you and your supporters who don't believe in spiritual beings, we probably seem like a cult.

Inside the Mind of President Biden a Week Before the Inauguration

BIDEN'S G.S.
I believe in spiritual things. I believe in spirits.

SHIO OKAWA
Well, if you look at the American mass media, they're at their "end."

BIDEN'S G.S.
They believe in spirits.

SHIO OKAWA
We can't trust them very much now.

BIDEN'S G.S.
They believe in spirits. They don't talk about it though because it's not good for their business.

SHIO OKAWA
Right now, very evil energy has entered Beijing and Beijing is using this energy to conquer the world. Only America could have stopped it. So the issue at hand is that Mr. Biden as president could weaken America.

BIDEN'S G.S.

You never know, you know. It's possible that Xi Jinping might become overly confident because I will be the president and that could lead him to his downfall.

SHIO OKAWA

Well, I hope that that might happen.

BIDEN'S G.S.

Yeah. We know that Beijing's economy is really just a bubble and it's just trying to make itself appear huge. So he'll make it seem as if he has power, leading to his downfall.

SHIO OKAWA

Well . . . okay.

BIDEN'S G.S.

Beijing has more than enough . . . Well, even if I don't become the president of the US, Beijing is despised enough by people by now. The world despises Beijing.

SHIO OKAWA

I see.

Inside the Mind of President Biden a Week Before the Inauguration

BIDEN'S G.S.
That's actually clearly true.

SHIO OKAWA
But he probably doesn't have the sensibility to realize that people despise him. Don't you think?

BIDEN'S G.S.
All the heads of state of Europe despise him now. They hate him, as they surely should. Just look at what he's done to Hong Kong. Now everyone's discovered what he's also done elsewhere. The truth about his concentration camps is known to them now, you know. To them, it's the nightmare of Hitler returning.

SHIO OKAWA
Well, it will be a good thing if Xi Jinping ends up taking bold actions to take advantage of Mr. Biden's weaknesses and by doing so, hidden truths about Xi Jinping get exposed.

BIDEN'S G.S.
There are numbers he's covering up.

SHIO OKAWA
Yes, yeah, yeah.

BIDEN'S G.S.
I know that there are. In comparison, America basically isn't able to conceal any information. So it's very difficult.

I mean, even though Beijing claims only several thousand deaths from the coronavirus, the actual number could be in the hundreds of thousands. You never know.

Biden's guardian spirit fears getting assassinated

SHIO OKAWA
Well, but you need to mitigate the impeachment charges. You might think it's fine as long as Mr. Trump gets crushed, but doing that could cause Trump "believers" to revolt even more.

BIDEN'S G.S.
Well, you might not be that interested in me. But your editorial division might have a lot of questions to ask me if you ask them because I'll become the next American president.

Inside the Mind of President Biden a Week Before the Inauguration

SHIO OKAWA

Then, that will be after you get through the inaugural ceremony safely and become the president.

BIDEN'S G.S.

Okay, okay. Hmmm.

SHIO OKAWA

Even if we ask you questions right away, you'll only talk about Trump and the usual things.

BIDEN'S G.S.

But aren't I going to get assassinated?

SHIO OKAWA

By who?

BIDEN'S G.S.

You people.

SHIO OKAWA

No.

BIDEN'S G.S.

Aren't you targeting me?

SHIO OKAWA

No, we're not. We don't have any guns anyway.

BIDEN'S G.S.

Hmmm. I'm suspicious of that.

SHIO OKAWA

Why? Of course we wouldn't assassinate you.

BIDEN'S G.S.

Because you could use black magic on me.

SHIO OKAWA

Master Okawa is very opposed to such kind of ideas.

BIDEN'S G.S.

Something like black magic.

SHIO OKAWA

We aren't going to assassinate you.

BIDEN'S G.S.
Okay, anyway.

SHIO OKAWA
It wouldn't be possible.

He'll listen to everyone else's opinions when he becomes the president

BIDEN'S G.S.
I just want you to say that I'm a nice person.

SHIO OKAWA
As I've been telling you, Happy Science has little influence as an opinion leader in America.

BIDEN'S G.S.
So in Japan... Let me see. Because Mr. Abe was in office for a long time, I don't know much about other prime ministers of the past. But if I were to tell you how nice I am as a person, I'm about as nice as Mr. Yoshiro Mori.

SHIO OKAWA

Even if you give us names of Japanese politicians, they're all about the same anyway.

BIDEN'S G.S.

I guess it's the same no matter who takes office.

SHIO OKAWA

But well, you're similar to Japanese people.

BIDEN'S G.S.

Yeah.

SHIO OKAWA

You're very Japanese.

BIDEN'S G.S.

Yeah, since I eat California rolls.

SHIO OKAWA

It will be like an experiment for what will happen if a Japanese person becomes the president of the US.

Inside the Mind of President Biden a Week Before the Inauguration

BIDEN'S G.S.
Yeah. So I'm not going to make decisions about anything. I'll just do things based on everyone else's opinion. That's what I'll be doing. Yes. What I mean is that I don't have my own opinion. Yes.

SHIO OKAWA
I see.

BIDEN'S G.S.
Yes.

SHIO OKAWA
Well, thank you very much then.

BIDEN'S G.S.
Okay. I'm sorry for coming in the middle of the night.

SHIO OKAWA
That's fine.

BIDEN'S G.S.
Because you, his wife, probably wouldn't be able to sleep, I thought it would be better for you to get some work done.

SHIO OKAWA
That's fine.

BIDEN'S G.S.
Since I've done a spiritual interview, Mr. Trump (his guardian spirit) will also want to come charging in, you know.

SHIO OKAWA
Right.

BIDEN'S G.S.
I think that you should have it during the daytime, as much as that's possible.

SHIO OKAWA
Okay. Goodbye.

BIDEN'S G.S.
Okay.

ENDNOTES

1 See Ryuho Okawa, *Spiritual Interviews with the Guardian Spirits of Biden and Trump* (Tokyo: HS Press, 2020).

2 Translator's Note: NHK is Japan's public media organization.

3 Yukio Hatoyama is a former prime minister of Japan (2009-2010) from the Democratic Party of Japan.

4 See Ryuho Okawa, *Spiritual Interview with the Guardian Spirit of Pope Francis* (Tokyo: HS Press, 2020).

5 Interviewer's Note: He is referring to my father, who lives in the suburbs.

CHAPTER TWO

How President Biden Will Deal with Critical Global Issues

*A Spiritual Interview with
Mr. Biden's Guardian Spirit—Part 2*

*Originally recorded in Japanese on January 20, 2021,
at the Special Lecture Hall of Happy Science in Japan
and later translated into English*

The four interviewers of this chapter are symbolized as A, B, C, and D.

1

A Look Inside the Mind of Mr. Biden

Looking into Biden's true character and thinking to forecast the coming four-year course of the world

RYUHO OKAWA

Good morning. It is 10:11 a.m. on January 20, 2021, in Japan. In terms of the time zone in Japan, Mr. Biden is scheduled to be inaugurated around dawn. It might have been better to hold this interview after watching the inaugural ceremony, but I'm certain that we'll hold another interview later. So, though it's still before the inaugural ceremony, I believe it's our job as Happy Science to forecast beforehand how America's course will change, how Japan's course will change, and how the world's course will change due to this new president of the US.

Last summer, we published[1] interviews with the guardian spirits of Mr. Biden and Mr. Trump that discussed the American presidential election. At that time, the first impression we got of Mr. Biden was not so good. On the other hand, Mr. Trump spoke with a lot of confidence. He asked us to add a tagline to the book that says, "God chose Trump to be president-elect!" Since we did as Mr. Trump requested, we'll also need to take a little bit of the responsibility for saying so. Our feeling was that owing to Mr. Trump's way of doing things, he would be easier to cooperate with. With 74 million votes that went to Mr. Trump and 81 million votes that went to Mr. Biden, *both* men got the highest number of votes in the history of US elections. So, there must have been a reason why Mr. Trump didn't easily concede until the very end.

At the same time, more than 80 million votes went to Mr. Biden, so there could be something all of these people are acknowledging about him. If there is something we've overlooked about him, then we should find it. Most importantly, though, we need to look inside at Mr. Biden's true character and ways of thinking so that we can see the course the world will take over these four or more years; we also want to forecast what kind of chess moves America's pieces will make so that we can develop our strategy. This sort of thing is what Happy Science can do. And well, since many, various people are involved when it comes to actually carrying them out, things may not go exactly as we desire. Since he's filled positions such as chairman of the Senate Foreign Relations Committee, many opinions say he's an expert in foreign diplomacy. But whether this expertise will really work beneficially or not is actually the biggest issue at hand.

[*Speaking to the interviewers*] I will leave the rest to you.

Mr. Biden's guardian spirit gets summoned and speaks his real thoughts

Let me summon him now. Since he spoke Japanese in the last interview, I think that he can also do so today. Except, it's possible he'll suddenly stop speaking in Japanese [*chuckles*] if your questions start to sound sharp. Considering that the majority of our viewers are Japanese, I'd like us to speak in Japanese as much as we can for their benefit.

[*Lightly claps his hands twice while speaking*] Now then, I would like to summon the guardian spirit of the 46th President of the United States, Joseph Biden.

Mr. Joseph Biden's guardian spirit, please come down to Happy Science to tell us what you're really thinking. Mr. Biden's guardian spirit, please speak to us.

[*About five seconds of silence pass.*]

2

Mr. Biden's State of Mind Shortly Before the Inaugural Ceremony

Biden's guardian spirit gets summoned and appears

BIDEN'S G.S.
[*Coughing*] Aaah, somehow.

A
Hello.

BIDEN'S G.S.
Somehow I'll manage to . . . I'm about to get the position.

A
Are you the guardian spirit of Mr. Biden?

BIDEN'S G.S.
I'm about to get the position somehow, without getting assassinated.

A

Yes. Today, we are about half a day away from your presidential inauguration.

BIDEN'S G.S.

Oh, you seem scary. Something about you feels that way.

A

Oh no, not at all.

BIDEN'S G.S.

I sense something about you, as if you're carrying a sword on your back.

A

No, no. This presidential election was very unprecedented in ...

BIDEN'S G.S.

Yes. It definitely was.

A

There are about 25,000 National Guardsmen on duty for the inaugural ceremony right now. Such a high state of alert during an inaugural ceremony is also unprecedented.

BIDEN'S G.S.
Mhm. Mhm. Mhm.

A
Also, you came to Master Ryuho Okawa about a week ago, on January 13, asking for a chance to give an official address.

BIDEN'S G.S.
Mhm. Yeah. I want to be able to give a really smart address. Yeah.

A
Yes. So, could you please let us hear it today?

BIDEN'S G.S.
At least you, who are here, won't be able to remove me from office. I'll stay in office as long as I don't die or I don't get defeated in the next election. Yeah.

He thinks that Trump is like King Kong

A
As you're now about to be inaugurated under such unprecedented, unusual circumstances, how do you honestly feel? And what kind of things are you thinking about right now?

BIDEN'S G.S.
Well, having Mr. Trump as president was as though we captured King Kong from a solitary south sea island, brought him to America, and put him into the White House. Since he's still alive, it's possible he could still go wild. We could put chains on him, but we still don't know what in the world he would do. That's one thing I could say.

Compared to him, I'm like Naomi Watts. My personality isn't considered dangerous by anyone and is really one that deserves to be loved.

So, there's King Kong after all. People don't know what he's talking about, you know. Twitter, Facebook, and various places have banned him because he's basically like a submarine that suddenly shoots torpedoes at you. After all, there are people who agree with and get incited by him. It's important not to let him say things, but he'd still be dangerous.

There are lots of American people who easily get angered by hearing unofficial information.

There's nothing inconvenient about someone as gentle as me becoming the president, so why does he have to say so much . . .? His personality of badmouthing anyone he sees should be fixed. It needs some religious fixing. You should bring him to Japan once and get him to practice self-reflection at Happy Science. Yeah.

A
On the other hand, seeing that 75 million people voted for Mr. Trump, do you feel that he was a formidable opponent for you?

BIDEN'S G.S.
Wait a minute, that was 1 million votes more than the actual number.

A
No, no [*laughs*]. I'm just speaking approximately.

BIDEN'S G.S.
He got 74 million votes. Yeah.

A

But actually, considering the various views you have been expressing, we haven't heard you talk about a clear policy. You've only been urging unity, not division, or urging Americans to come together.

BIDEN'S G.S.

The news media in Japan, America, and the rest of the world have been basically saying that about me. It feels like I've already done my job just by accomplishing that. Yeah. I've done my job just by being in this position.

As for Mr. Trump, he just rips things to shreds. He does wild things again and again.

The president is a symbol after all. He's just the symbol of the country's union. That's all he needs to be. Yeah.

He says that Kamala Harris was chosen just to gather votes from women and Black people

A

I have some questions from a journalistic standpoint.

BIDEN'S G.S.
Okay, ah, uhuh, uhuh.

A
People are already saying that you could be the weakest president since Jimmy Carter. Do you have any objections to that?

BIDEN'S G.S.
Okay, I'm thankful to hear that. Go ahead and say so because that way, my approval ratings can only go upward. So they can go right ahead and say so. Yeah. Go on, go on. Because when I do something, my score will only go higher. Yeah.

A
To be frank with you, some people believe that a second term could be very difficult for you to win.

BIDEN'S G.S.
Well, you never know. You never know. Sometimes I can be very persistent. Yeah. Maybe that "maybe" might happen. Because, in some cases, it's the person with less greed who wins, you know.

A

There are also opinions saying that Vice President Kamala Harris might replace you, depending on the circumstances. What are your thoughts about that?

BIDEN'S G.S.

Hmmm, well, the purpose of having Ms. Harris on the ticket was to gather votes from women and Black people. So I don't think that she has the capability of being president in actual reality. Things won't work unless I'm the president. Mhm. For now. For now, okay?

A

Meaning you're confident about yourself.

His view on foreign diplomacy is that as many people as possible should be friends

A

Master Okawa also mentioned about this earlier. Is it true that you believe foreign diplomacy is your strongest area?

BIDEN'S G.S.

Well, we've gotten isolated, you know, so I've got to tear down the "Trump Isolation" that we've been going through. Foreign diplomacy is about getting as many people as possible to be friends with each other. You're not really supposed to create enemies, especially if you're the strongest country in the world, like America is. Creating enemies carelessly would be the same as bullying the weak. That's something that we shouldn't really do, yeah.

A

Until now, President Trump has been prioritizing bilateral negotiations over other things.

BIDEN'S G.S.

He can only do things by himself.

A

Yes, he didn't regard international organizations or the United Nations that highly. What is the kind of future vision you have with regard to this area?

BIDEN'S G.S.

Well, he mostly made decisions based on whether something has gains or benefits. That's how people in business or how business executives make decisions. But politics is a non-profit enterprise. So, well, there are things we need to do regardless of whether they benefit us. That's politics. In other words, politics does things that company executives can't do, you know.

So, for example, if something leads to maintaining good relations with the world, it's important for us to suffer some damages to help the weak people, even if doing so won't bring us benefit or will mean we'll suffer losses. From an international standpoint, it would become a problem after all if a huge superpower such as the US isolates itself from the world, don't you think so? Mr. Trump must have been aiming to surround China and isolate Beijing from the rest of the world. But what happened instead of that was the opposite; America became isolated from the world and is getting thrown out. This is the reason why the mass media had good reason to think that they need Biden to become the president. Yeah.

The reason he showed support for LGBT people

A
All the major news media of America have been very nice to you. They've basically been your cheerleading squad.

BIDEN'S G.S.
Yeah, they must see me as a light of angel. I'm sure of that.

A
In the area of domestic politics, you've gained some attention for appointing women and LGBT people. For example, you've appointed Peter Buttigieg to a cabinet position. It's, well, very typical of the Democratic Party to do things like increase diversity and appeal to minority groups.

BIDEN'S G.S.
Well, I had to do that, you see. Because, in the beginning, even I was just a minor candidate. That's why by showing that I'm willing to accept minorities, I started becoming a mainstream candidate. So that's something you have to do. You see?

It doesn't exactly agree with my ways of thinking. It doesn't. But it's part of my job to make compromises, to some extent, and accept some things that I don't agree with because there are many kinds of American people and we must accept every citizen who pays taxes to our country. Yeah.

3
Finding Out His Strategy Against China

He's planning to negotiate with China enough to avoid war

B

Earlier, Master Okawa said . . .

BIDEN'S G.S.

Wait a minute—why are you wearing a tie that's almost red (the color of the Republican Party)?

B

I tried to be polite and switched it to a pink one to lean a little bit toward blue.

BIDEN'S G.S.

But your Master has "obediently" worn a blue one. [*Pointing to Interviewer C*] Look, he's also wearing a red one. [*Pointing to Interviewer A*] And him, too! So you're all supporters of the Republicans, aren't you?

B

Master Okawa said, earlier, that because you're an expert in foreign diplomacy, this is the area where there will be issues. So I'd like to get to discussing the core issues regarding foreign diplomacy.

BIDEN'S G.S.
Hmmm. Okay.

B

There was mention of China. When you came to us just a week ago, you said that you'll pretend to put pressure on Beijing.

BIDEN'S G.S.
Mhm.

B

You, Mr. Biden's guardian spirit, said that that's what you're going to pretend to do but that actually you're going to change America's intended enemy from Beijing to the Kremlin. You told us that these are things you intend to do.[2]

BIDEN'S G.S.
Okay. Okay.

B
You, the guardian spirit, told us about this.

BIDEN'S G.S.
Okay. Okay. Okay.

B
Could you give us more details on your thinking behind that?

BIDEN'S G.S.
Well, if you look at things from the opposite side, you'll see that a war will start with China if you let Trump continue for four more years as president. So it's about whether we want that to happen or not. If we go to war on top of this coronavirus disaster that's creating worldwide suffering, numerous sick people, and a high number of deaths, there will be more and more tragedy. Of course, there will be damage to our people and to their people, and it will also impact other countries.

This is why I said those things in that way—that we should basically hold negotiations to the degree that we can avoid going to war.

B

If you plan to take a "basically peaceful" stance, people around the world will be very worried about America's position weakening to a great extent against Beijing, who is basically using military force to determine everything now. What are your thoughts regarding that?

BIDEN'S G.S.

What I think regarding that is, weeeeell... that's something that the "chairman of the Joint Chiefs of Staff" should think about. Yeah.

He says there's no use in investigating the real source of the coronavirus

B

But before you delegate that issue to the military, you have some important issues to consider. You said, just now, that you want to avoid going to war as much as possible and also mentioned an even larger issue: that you want to avoid war so that Americans won't die. But the death toll in America due to the coronavirus is higher than the death toll that resulted from World War II.

BIDEN'S G.S.
Mhm. Mhm. Mhm.

B
When you visited us a week ago, you told us you've never given thought to where the coronavirus could have come from. Or, to be more specific, you told us you don't want to find out the answer to that. You went on to tell us why you feel this way and said that a nuclear war with China could occur if the world discovers that the coronavirus was developed in a Chinese laboratory, which then got released or was deliberately spread, causing millions of people in America and around the world to die. You continued by saying that you don't want that to be what actually happened and that because you don't want to hear that conclusion, there's no need to find out where the coronavirus originally came from. You had said these things to us just a week ago. Could you tell us how you feel about this?

BIDEN'S G.S.

The idea of organizing relief activities to save infected people's lives and the idea of using weapons to kill numerous people can't come from the same person at the same time. If you desire to save people, then you need to save people. Doing such kind of conflicting things might be possible if there is worldwide acknowledgment that something is overwhelmingly evil. But should we ever enter into war with China, we'll need all the European and Asian countries to reach a consensus after all. Even America doesn't intend to go to war unless we can do that.

Not adding further suffering to suffering is what the mainstream news media has been insisting on. I don't think we should misread their voice.

Now, with regard to my intent to change America's intended enemy to Russia, I'll say that Trump's scandal with Russia was a topic being talked about even before he got inaugurated. And well, he's done various things such as pardon people as he likes with regard to that issue, you know. If he had won this term, I would've been the one thrown into prison for my scandal with China. So, well, you can't tell which is which. In a powerful country like America, you'll have many connections with other countries. So, sometimes you'll get accused of various wrongs when you fall on the defeated side. But at least I hope that America doesn't start resembling a country like South Korea.

And . . . what were you trying to say? Were you saying it's wrong of me to avoid finding out where the coronavirus originated from?

B
I'm asking why you don't want to.

BIDEN'S G.S.
It's because the virus has already spread all over the world to the point of infecting 100 million people. Whatever we say won't change anything about that now, and Beijing is not going to be persuaded. They're trying to say things such as, "It originated from America" or "It originated from Europe." And because of the recent theory of bats being the virus' origin, Beijing is now saying, in addition to many other things, that the coronavirus spread to bats from minks or that it directly came from minks.

B
Well, even the World Health Organization is denying those things.

BIDEN'S G.S.
Whatever we do is of no use. Even if we said anything, they're not going to admit anything. Things will only become a mud-slinging contest.

Looking at how much he knows about where the coronavirus came from

B
With the inauguration being imminent, I see that you've come here prepared enough to have a congressional debate, unlike a week ago.

BIDEN'S G.S.
Of course. Of course I've properly . . . that's precisely the reason I asked you (to let me have a spiritual interview).

B
I have a question I was planning to ask you during the later half of the interview . . .

BIDEN'S G.S.
Mister, I'll remind you that you're talking to the president, you know. Even the news media has to submit their questions to me beforehand.

B
Yes. Of course I'm asking you these questions politely, just as a reporter from FOX News or CNN would.

BIDEN'S G.S.
Okay. Mhm. Okay.

B
On that note, you just said that the coronavirus has already spread and there's nothing we can do about it. I'd like to talk about that. A week ago, you revealed it's possible that the US government already knows of the possible second and third waves of the virus coming.

BIDEN'S G.S.
Oh. Well, variants of it have appeared one after another at a pace of one new variant every couple of weeks, you know.

B

No, no, it wasn't about the virus' variants. I'm asking you this question because when you spoke to us a week ago, you said that you don't want to think about where the coronavirus came from and that you don't want to find out the answer to that because if you do, there will be a lot of trouble. Many of the people who heard you say that got the impression that you actually already know where it came from.

BIDEN'S G.S.

Even if you destroyed China right now, the coronavirus itself isn't going to disappear. It's already spread around the world, you know. A different type of it is spreading in Brazil, a different type of it is also spreading in the UK, and there are many other types. This issue can't be fixed anymore. That's why I'm saying that if we have time to hold a mud-slinging contest, we should work on establishing a relief system first.

B

Since there are religious solutions for dispelling the coronavirus, we, Happy Science, will think about that separately. So, as I was saying, we got the impression from the last time we spoke with you that you already know about the source.

And you told us further details about it. Actually, it wasn't just the last time. You also talked about it in the book that's right in front of you,[3] which we published in August.

BIDEN'S G.S.
Oh. Ah, okay.

B
So, I felt that you must really want to tell us about it.

BIDEN'S G.S.
Well, after I'm inaugurated as president, I don't think that I'm going to say America was involved with it. I'm not going to say anything about that. Not anymore, not anymore.

B
By saying, "Not anymore," you're admitting that what you've talked about before is true.

BIDEN'S G.S.
I'm not talking about it anymore [*laughs*]. Of course I can't possibly talk about that. If I do, we'd have to take responsibility.

He insists on starting discussions regarding the mass massacres in Uyghur from a blank slate

B
In other words, what's crucial here is that as the president of the United States, you're admitting that you'll assist in concealing the wrongdoings committed by Beijing. You're admitting that this is going to be the current president-elect's stance.

BIDEN'S G.S.
Assist...? Assist...?

B
You're admitting that you're going to conceal the truth about where the coronavirus originated from and why it spread because doing so is actually also in the interests of the United States of America. Is it alright if we consider this the official stance of the president of the United States?

BIDEN'S G.S.
Well, I need to show a clear difference between Trump and myself for now because Trump is doing all that he can until

the very last minute. It's already the day before the inauguration and he's still talking about the massacres in Uyghur, trying to leave me with homework. He's practically trying to leave behind a volatile situation right before leaving office.

Anyway, when I take office, I'll need to negotiate things or, I mean, discuss things based on a blank slate. If there are massacres being committed in Uyghur, then I'll first need to send in a team there to investigate. That would be the modern and scientific way to handle that issue, I think. So we will need to do that. And if Beijing denies us from investigating, then I guess I should apply pressure on Beijing. I can't just continue where the previous president has left off. Changing presidents would have no meaning to it if I did that.

In any case, if we keep going at the same rate as we are now, we're walking straight into a war. That is the way this feels. Is this alright with you? Is this alright with Japan? That's the question.

He reveals that the coronavirus research started in the US

B
If you keep going at the same rate as you are now, China will take concrete action after the presidential transition. For example, we've seen signs in Taiwan and Hong Kong about that. I'd like to get into this topic a little later. But before we do, I'd like to return to the current topic one more time and check with you about something. Some news sources like Newsweek have reported on this topic already: biological weapons have an indistinguishable dual-use nature of having beneficial medicinal uses but also harmful uses as weapons. A week ago, you told us that the American and Chinese militaries were actually jointly conducting coronavirus research but that America withdrew on realizing how dangerous it can be. But China carried on and eventually completed the research. Because this has already been released, our readers and viewers can also read or watch that spiritual message.

BIDEN'S G.S.
Hmm.

B
And you also said that it would be bad for the US if this issue is revealed and that because you don't want that to happen, you want to avoid dealing with this issue. You said that it doesn't matter if China supposedly created the coronavirus inside a laboratory and then spread it around the world and that you just want to leave it at that. Do you still feel the same way?

BIDEN'S G.S.
Well, a part of your information is wrong. You described that China and America were conducting joint research in China and then America withdrew while China continued. But there was something before that. Yeah. Actually, the research was started in America and because the Chinese scientist returned to China, the American scientist also went to China so they could continue the research together. But realizing how dangerous the research was, the American scientist withdrew from it. So, it originally...

B
It had started in the US.

BIDEN'S G.S.
The research started in the US, not China.

B
So, you're saying that it's worse.

BIDEN'S G.S.
Because China would want to say that the research began in America, it would become a mud-slinging contest and get quite bad. That's why I said that it's something we shouldn't get into.

B
Okay. Actually, that's what my second question is about. The US backed out of the research in 2014 because of several accidents that occurred. The last time we spoke, you said that for 15 years, a joint research was being conducted. Considering this fact, we thought that for about a decade prior to 2014, starting in 2005, America wasn't alone in conducting the coronavirus research. This is a huge global scoop that no one has yet discovered, and I was quite surprised. But do you now mean to say that America was actually conducting the research alone?

BIDEN'S G.S.
Wait, you. You're out of line. Countries owning nuclear weapons might be putting more into their nuclear weapons programs. But all the countries that don't have them—other than the extremely underdeveloped ones—are conducting bioweapons and virus-weapons research. I'm not sure about Japan . . . well, actually, yes, this includes Japan and other moderately advanced countries. If you really want to look into it, you'll discover that countries like Iran and Iraq also own bioweapons. Everyone is in possession of something like that.

He is planning on developing mutually supportive diplomatic negotiations with China

B
That's actually not the topic I wanted to ask you, a Democratic president, about today. Exactly as you said, America backed out in 2014. But people discovered that the previous US Democratic administration was funding China while it was continuing its coronavirus research. People have been angered and been wanting an explanation about that.

Am I right that you don't want the public to know that the US administration at that time—which was the Obama administration—was funding the development of the coronavirus? And is this the reason you're trying to avoid the issue?

BIDEN'S G.S.
Well, but that's what we do in foreign diplomacy. Listen, well, it's true that China achieved a lot of growth during the Obama administration. In addition to that, China aimed to double the size of its 2010 G.D.P. by 2020. So in order to develop its country, it increased foreign trade, increased domestic demand, and expanded into many foreign countries.

Also, America was going through a recession already. When Mr. Obama came to office, we were already in the second great depression. America needed to save itself; so, since China was growing at that time, Mr. Obama thought that being friends with China will let America coexist and prosper together with China.

Even if China had been conducting research that could, by chance, produce that kind of a biological weapon, there shouldn't be any issues as long as America is friends with China.

A
You're known by everyone as an expert in foreign diplomacy. And that part of you makes us feel that you must be very knowledgeable regarding the extremely deep, concealed aspects of the US–China relations.

BIDEN'S G.S.
Well, yeah. I am, of course. There are things that I know about.

That's the reason why I don't want to put China at a disadvantage . . . because Beijing is also supporting my son. There's a mutual relationship between us, like the mutually supportive relationship that Japanese people like to have.

He will let Japan and China compete in a "sumo match" and will take the winner's side

A
Well, when we tried to think about the course things can take from now on and we looked at your relationships with China, we noticed your friendliness toward Mr. Xi Jinping. For example, you personally hosted Mr. Xi Jinping when he

visited the US (in 2012). Also, during your vice presidency, Mr. Xi Jinping received you with a lot of hospitality during your visit to China. People around the world are paying the closest attention to this topic of how you view Mr. Xi Jinping. Could you tell us about that?

BIDEN'S G.S.
Well, he must probably be a champion of a great developing country, whereas we're an advanced country. He must be someone with tremendous power as a champion of a developing country.

But it's my basic understanding that America is at least 50 years ahead of China right now. We could share our technology with them or they could steal it from us. On the other hand, China doesn't have anything we would want to steal from them. Our relationship with them is like a champion sumo wrestler who is offering their shoulders to the others. So I wasn't so worried about them. Our basic strategy was to restrain Japan and China while making them compete with each other.

A
Do you mean that you don't necessarily favor either of them over the other . . . ?

BIDEN'S G.S.

... let them compete with each other, and we also encourage other Asian countries to develop their economies.

Well, our basic strategy is to maintain balance so that all hegemonic control won't fall into the hands of one unitary country. So, whenever China became too strong, we've created competition by encouraging Japan to also grow.

B

With regard to this, last time you revealed another honest thought that you have. Actually, people related to the Department of Defense uniformly agree that many areas of China's military strength have nearly reached America's level. In such a high-pressure situation, it's possible that a war or a conflict could erupt. Regarding this, you, Mr. Biden's guardian spirit, have said that you'll be fine if war breaks out between China and America but that you want to keep the battleground within Japan. These words were not spoken by me but by you, Mr. Biden's guardian spirit.[4]

You just now said that you'll preserve the balance between Japan and China. At the same time, however, you have told us that when conflict erupts, you'll direct the damage toward Japan. You said that this is the overall strategy

America has—a crucial point that the Japanese administration should know about.

BIDEN'S G.S.
Your words are starting to sound like Latin to me. I can't hear what you're saying anymore. I've been trying to listen to you in Japanese but can't understand the context of your words that well now.

B
No, no. You're capable of speaking Japanese very fluently, so please let us talk in Japanese.

BIDEN'S G.S.
Aah? Hmmm.

B
You said that if confrontation erupts, you want Japan to become the battleground and try to end the conflict here.

BIDEN'S G.S.
Your Japanese is hard for me to understand. I could catch only half of what you said. Well, it must feel the same way to you when you're watching CNN.

B

Put simply, you said that if you were forced to choose between China and Japan, you will choose China in the end.

BIDEN'S G.S.

No, I'll make China and Japan duke it out in a sumo match and I'll side with the winner.

B

You'll make China and Japan wrestle each other?

BIDEN'S G.S.

We'll hold a fair sumo match between them. America will referee this match and determine the winner.

B

America and Japan are allies. But you're going to make us fight a match with China in spite of that? And then you'll side with the winner?

BIDEN'S G.S.

We have a military alliance with Japan, but we've been aiming to develop an economic alliance with China. So it's complicated.

Inside the Mind of President Biden

He doesn't see that it's possible for China to gain hegemonic control

A
Regarding the relationship between America and China, Master Ryuho Okawa has told us that the possibility of China gaining hegemonic control has sped up tremendously. Previously, a possible scenario saw America getting outrun by China around the year 2035. But it's possible that in reality, this will already happen this very year, in 2021.

BIDEN'S G.S.
Well, there are various ways that this can be looked at. Ever since the Lehman crisis of 2008, Japan also received America's impact and went through tough times since then. Because of the great difficulty of recovering from that recession, there was even a change of administration to the minority party, leading to a lot of dependence on China.

Well, America also needed to get some wealth from China to bounce back from the recession after all. We required a great deal of help from China in this way during Obama's presidency. So if Beijing wants to become our ally, I'll take advantage of that offer. And if Beijing wants to become our enemy, then I'll need to rethink the situation.

How President Biden Will Deal with Critical Global Issues

You can overestimate China's military strength as much as you want to, but a truly strong country wouldn't work on developing biological weapons in this day and age. That's what a weak country like North Korea would actually be working on because when a nuclear war erupts, North Korea could try firing a missile, but an enemy's counter-fire at it would definitely destroy it.

(But their use of bioweapons,) would make them unidentifiable as the source. North Korea could use bioweapons while denying that fact, making it impossible to determine that North Korea did it and leaving the enemy without a clear, just reason for a counterassault on North Korea.

Compared to this, if North Korea were ever to fire a single nuclear missile at, say, Guam—because Guam has been supporting Trump—then America can counter-fire with a combination of ten shots, bringing North Korea to its end. This is why I've never thought of bioweapons as advanced weapons.

It could make a circle and come back to you like now ... It's a little unbelievable that China's death toll has been so low, but unless you're like Japan during the isolationist period, you wouldn't be capable of completely blocking out the virus from your own country.

So, well, what I'm trying to say is that while I am in office, I'll take advantage of China as much as I can . . . and how do I say this, I don't see the possibility of China gaining hegemonic control.

4

Asking Him about Coronavirus Measures and Environmental Issues

He believes that the coronavirus is a "god of good luck" that drove out Trump

A

Another big factor we need to think about, actually, is the negative impact that the coronavirus has had on the economy and the fact that you and your advisors have been planning measures that are completely opposite to Trumponomics. For example, you're going to increase taxes heavily. But the world isn't clearly aware that doing so could lead to a huge recession. How confident do you feel . . .

BIDEN'S G.S.

What in the world are you saying? It was all thanks to the coronavirus that Trump got defeated. What a blessing it's been. The coronavirus has been like a god of good luck.

A

Have you thought about what's going to happen from now on...?

BIDEN'S G.S.

Four hundred thousand people did die.[5] But it's thanks to the coronavirus that a "happy future" has come to America because now we can send King Kong back to an isolated southern island.

B

Due to the lockdowns, annual economic growth is now below minus 30 percent. It's the first time this has happened since the Great Depression. Is this what a happy future looks like to you?

BIDEN'S G.S.

That happened all because of Trump's stupidity. Since the New York City mayor was a Democrat, he kept insisting on a lockdown. But Trump refused to issue one, saying that it's not a national-level issue and therefore everyone should decide what to do independently. So, it's completely Trump's responsibility.

Even though people insisted that he should issue one, he told the states to decide for themselves. He didn't listen and didn't handle it at the federal level, saying that it's not a national-level issue. This led to taking many months to handle it.

In the midst of this, he was fully confident that he'll win the election against me and he just kept going. His great pride is responsible for this; also, his blindness is responsible for this. He won't do something if it will only result in incurring expenses. But that means he didn't understand how politics works. Politics is essentially a non-profit enterprise. Over the four years he was in office, he failed to understand this aspect of politics.

His idea of a coronavirus measure is the use of masks, disinfectants, and vaccines

C
Vaccines are being created one after another right now. But in that case…

BIDEN'S G.S.
Vaccines will bring us a little profit, so that's a good thing.

C
Vaccinations are being given widely now. But if people realize that they're not effective and new variants of the virus keep appearing and spreading, increasing the number of infections, is your administration planning to issue a lockdown?

BIDEN'S G.S.
Hmm . . . well for the time being, this is a time of experimenting to see if using masks, disinfectants, and vaccines will let us survive—although I don't know if you could call this method completely scientific. Trump reacted too slowly. So I'm now testing how that will work out. Since he didn't have any ideas or plans and has done nothing, he can't blame other people for his defeat.

C
But during Mr. Trump's presidency, vaccine development progressed very quickly. When Mr. Biden got his vaccination, even he complimented the Trump administration for their successful job.

BIDEN'S G.S.
Actually, the pharmaceutical companies weren't supportive of Trump. In fact, the vaccines were nearly ready, and Mr. Trump had wanted to say, "We'll give 100 million vaccinations in 100 days," like I've done. But in order to ensure Trump was defeated in the election, the pharmaceutical companies didn't tell him that the vaccines were ready. Then, when the election was over and I got elected, they suddenly announced that the vaccines are ready.

So it was the people's will to get rid of him. You can't do anything about that. So we needed to mostly disinfect ourselves of Trump himself. Yeah.

Taxes from the wealthy class and large corporations will fund his 2-trillion dollar coronavirus measure

B
Let's put this issue about the pharmaceutical companies aside and go back to the point at hand. What you have said just now shows us that the blue states will face another lock-

down recession and a huge recession during Biden's presidency. We can clearly see that happening.

BIDEN'S G.S.
How? A recession hasn't even come yet.

B
No, no. That kind of future is going to...

BIDEN'S G.S.
We've already put out a 200-trillion yen (2-trillion dollar) measure even before Biden has taken office.

B
That will become an issue. You'll require a way to finance it. In other words, it's a measure that relies on huge tax increases. It's going to heavily...

BIDEN'S G.S.
Isn't that a good thing?

B
I was actually hoping you would admit to believing that it's a good thing.

BIDEN'S G.S.

Only very few people own 99 percent of the wealth, you know. [*Pointing to C*] All the people in companies like the one that you previously worked for possess loads of money, so of course we have to extract money from such kinds of people. They're loaded with money. So we need to just "extract" it from them and then redistribute that money to the people who are struggling. This is what Jesus Christ truly wants us to do. Do you see?

B

President Biden, I understand that what you just said is a campaign tactic of yours. I see that you're trying to gather votes from the masses or, should I say, the left-leaning people. But do you mean that your philosophy or way of thinking as the president of the United States is that extracting taxes from people owning 99 percent of the wealth and then distributing this wealth to others will basically solve the problem?

BIDEN'S G.S.

Well . . . well, I'm not certain about the exact number. But I think it is about 20 percent of the people who own 99 percent of the wealth. Yeah. And it is probably about 1 percent of the people who own 70 or 80 percent of the wealth. Well, I don't know the exact numbers. The people with jobs related to Wall Street own most of the wealth, in other words.

So, well, if you calculate things purely based on profit versus loss, then you'd insist that jobless Mexican immigrants living in near-slum conditions should be ignored. Since they don't have money to get vaccinations, you could say that we should let them die. This is what you would say if you're only thinking in terms of profit versus loss. That's Trump's way of looking at things.

But if we try to give vaccines to everyone without that kind of thinking, then we'll need some way to pay for it. So, of course, we should extract this money from people who own more wealth than necessary, people who don't need all of their money.

He will drive Trump to the point of needing to sell the Trump Tower

B
Okay. A public commitment was made to raise taxes on the wealthy class. And then . . .

BIDEN'S G.S.

Yes. That should be a natural thing to do. It's something that Jesus Christ approves, too.

B

I see. You feel it's only natural to implement that measure.

BIDEN'S G.S.

That measure has received a stamp of approval, yeah.

B

Okay, you think that it's only natural to do so.

In addition to that measure, there are plans to increase the taxes on large corporations. Is this also something you believe is only natural to do as a public commitment or as something even more important than that?

BIDEN'S G.S.

Yeah. I'm definitely going all the way until the Trump Tower needs to be sold off.

B

You're planning on going that far?

BIDEN'S G.S.

Yeah. I'll drive him to the point he'll need to sell it off. We don't need it as a symbol of New York anymore.

B

We should do our best to inform American economists about that.

BIDEN'S G.S.

I'm going to keep going until Trump is driven into debt and has to sell off the Trump Tower. Yeah.

C

So, let's imagine that financial wealth gets successfully extracted and the 200-trillion yen (2-trillion dollar) measure gets implemented. Does President Biden believe widespread vaccinations will end the spread of the coronavirus?

BIDEN'S G.S.

Yes, of course. Well, if people would have worn their masks more frequently, the coronavirus wouldn't have spread as much as it has. How embarrassing it is to be an advanced nation but have the highest number of infected people. We also caused Japan a lot of trouble. The Olympics had to be canceled because of this. You see?

C
Then, have you not thought about what to do if the coronavirus doesn't stop spreading?

BIDEN'S G.S.
If the coronavirus doesn't stop spreading, then because many lawsuit charges against China are being made now, I'll get Beijing to pay us.

He believes that investing in environmental preservation won't lead to a great depression

A
The conversation on environmental issues is another major factor in economic policymaking. Mr. Biden announced he'll rejoin the Paris climate accord the very day that he gets inaugurated and that he'll also shut down fracking. Fracking was something Mr. Trump had been supporting.

BIDEN'S G.S.

Well, fracking is a useless, high-cost industry, you know. They drill 2,000 meters downwards into the ground and then make a turn to further drill horizontally. Trump was supporting fracking for the job creation it brings, but that's now just a dated idea.

A

Mr. Suga, the prime minister of Japan, also announced that there'll be a shift in the same direction. The world seems to be trending in that direction.

BIDEN'S G.S.

Which direction are you talking about? Do you mean "toward following environmentalism"?

A

Yes. Toward investments in green energy, for example.

BIDEN'S G.S.

It can't be helped, I guess, since everyone is talking about it. Going against things like that will mean losing the support of the mass media and getting thrown out of office. That's how it works. As a politician, all you can do is let the mass media take responsibility for what happens later.

A
But the thing is, people have raised concern that environmentalism could become a major cause of the next huge economic recession, a global depression.

BIDEN'S G.S.
But environmentalism will require the development of a lot of new technologies and skills and lead to new businesses getting created that way. If policies following environmentalism are handled well, I think that they could improve the economy, since it will mean everyone will have to make the shift to it, too.

Several decades ago, Japan also faced issues regarding industrial pollution. Factories were dumping their waste water into rivers, leading to hordes of fish dying, people's bones bending, and people getting the Itai-itai disease. Corporations were dumping their waste material into rivers to avoid incurring costs and being in the red. The same thing is happening in China right now. Yeah. People there can't source their drinking water from the rivers anymore.

We need to make sure that corporations prevent that kind of pollution, even if it costs them money. If you want companies to survive in the future, you need to make corporations aware that they won't survive unless they're kind to people. I think 70 to 80 percent of people will agree with me on that.

A
Well, actually, Ms. Greta is a good representation of this issue. Are you aware that this issue is a conspiracy to destroy the economies of the advanced countries of the world?

BIDEN'S G.S.
That can't be true. How could someone so young who is purely asking people to protect her future . . .

B
Before we get to discussing the conspiracy theory, you've just clearly shown us that you're completely overestimating the success of technological developments in wind and solar energy, as you intend to end the use of energy sources such as nuclear power, oil, and coal. We now understand that you don't have the right judgment. Based on that, we now

How President Biden Will Deal with Critical Global Issues

understand the dangerous situation that America will be facing going forward.

5

On Peace in Asia and His Value Judgments on Justice

He thinks that it's only natural for Hong Kong to be eventually assimilated by China

B

Since people around the world are, in a sense, eager to know the content of this interview, I'd like to shift our topic of discussion from problems about America's economy back to issues related to foreign diplomacy. My first question is related to a topic that people in Japan and around the world are especially concerned about: the situation in Hong Kong.

BIDEN'S G.S.

Hong Kong?

B

Yes. People want to know how the new American President will handle the situation in Hong Kong. When news of Mr. Biden's likelihood to get elected spread, we saw a flurry of arrests happen one after another. The human rights and democracy of the Hong Kong people are in danger right now, to say the least. Could you tell us how Mr. Biden plans to deal with this situation?

BIDEN'S G.S.
Well, anyway, distinguishing the large issues from the small ones is important to do. Is it politically righteous to help 7 million Hong Kong people preserve their living conditions, even at the cost of 1.4 billion people (of China) coming under war's harm? Or, since Hong Kong will get assimilated into China anyway, is it better to counsel Hong Kong toward holding discussions and carefully negotiating toward a smooth transition?

When I saw the mob rioting at the Capitol building, I could sympathize with why Beijing wants to suppress the Hong Kong people's riots. Beijing must feel the same way that I did.

B
Well, human rights diplomacy is a major policy of the American Democratic Party. It's only a matter of time before the people of Hong Kong face huge suppression. It

could happen at any moment. Are you saying that when it does, you're going to look the other way?

BIDEN'S G.S.
Yeah. No, well...

B
Then, you're going to look the other way about the "small issue"—of protecting Hong Kong from getting destroyed—so that you can preserve the "big issue" of protecting economic ties with Beijing?

BIDEN'S G.S.
This is a chance for Japan, actually. Hong Kong's economy was ranked third in the world after New York's and London's financial markets. But everyone's trying to escape from Hong Kong now because Xi Jinping's failure in managing the economy crippled Hong Kong's international financial market. This means if Tokyo seizes this market, Japan can regain prosperity. This is your chance! Since this is a chance I'm giving you, you should be jumping at it!

B
Well, we'll think about that another time.

He feels that putting pressure on Beijing is enough to handle the genocide in Uyghur

B
Continuing the topic of Hong Kong, the same kind of trouble facing Hong Kong is also facing elsewhere in mainland China. These regions include Uyghur, South Mongolia, and Tibet. Particularly with regards to Uyghur, former Secretary of State Pompeo stated publicly during the administration-transition process that Beijing is committing genocide especially in Uyghur. Then, the newly appointed secretary of state also stated to Congress, yesterday, that he's very much in agreement with Mr. Pompeo's view.

This means that President Biden's secretary of state publicly stated his decision to continue the same policy. In Uyghur, Beijing is conducting what's very close to a mass genocide right now. How are you planning to handle this issue?

BIDEN'S G.S.
Well, people know that a huge massacre was committed in China during Mao Zedong's era. There was mass massacre of tens of millions to hundreds of millions of people—deaths numbered a hundred million or even two hundred million. But right now, I can't refuse to acknowledge the Chinese

Communist Party based on the mass genocide it committed during its establishment. The same goes for the Soviet Union. During Lenin's and Stalin's rule, the Soviets might have committed mass massacres. But we can't use this reason to refuse relationships with the current Russian government.

There was also a time like that in America—during the period of slavery. People bought slaves from Africa and used them for labor. This wasn't the same as genocide, but it was still a very cruel thing to do to Africa. African countries can sue America about that and demand compensation worth hundreds of years of this sinful deed, the way South Korea demands (the same thing from Japan). If Africa did that, America would have to pay them. This kind of thing happens to all advanced countries, so we have to start from scratch again. We have to rethink things from zero again.

B
In other words, are you saying that nothing can be done about the genocide in Uyghur? Is that your conclusion?

BIDEN'S G.S.
No, well, because we're applying pressure on Beijing, it's trying to disguise things as much as possible. Right? So

Beijing is saying things like, "That's not what we're doing. We are educating the people of Uyghur, just reeducating them. They're just being taught about the Chinese laws, language, and other educational things like that. Some of the people are even commuting from home."

The international community will be looking at this situation. Look at what happened with Wuhan. A year later, WHO finally sent people in to investigate the situation there. Since Beijing knows that there will eventually be an investigation, they know that they need to clean things up. So I think that applying pressure will give enough encouragement toward change.

I don't think we should use (what you said) as a reason to go to war, the way that Trump would want to, or destroy China's economy down to its very roots, or do rough things like that. All of the major newspapers will support my way of thinking.

He says that he can't intervene into other countries' domestic affairs past a certain line

B
Well, I'll put aside the genocide cases of 100,000 to 200,000 people and tell you that when the number of deaths due to genocide reaches millions or tens of millions, it will reach the level of Hitler's massacres. I'll represent worldwide public opinion and tell you that handling Beijing in the way you just described won't be enough. People around the world right now are sounding this alarm. Could you please comment on that as the president of America?

BIDEN'S G.S.
Okay, but Beijing has another way of thinking. For example, due to the Dalai Lama's weak ability in politics, Tibet faced a lot of famine and poverty. Then, when Beijing advanced into Tibet and laid a kind of bullet-train railway leading there, Tibetans saw new jobs being created and the standard of living getting better for everyone. So now, the Tibetans have abandoned old superstitions and they want to work in new, future-oriented industries.

Beijing is telling Uyghur to also join China and that Uyghur will be forgiven for trespassing upon the Great

Wall and attacking them in the past. It's the same as when Americans reconciled with the Native Americans. The Native Americans went through genocide, too. But by Americanizing themselves, they could survive, whereas not doing so could have led to their destruction.

Across the histories around the world, such things occurred at times. But at least because the world's eyes are watching, we will need to think about a soft landing. Well, I guess since human rights diplomacy is supposed to be a motto of the Democratic Party, I will follow that.

But I don't see why we should help Uyghur at the cost of waging war. What good could the Uyghur people do? What sort of influence could they have on the world? All they're doing is trying to get help from others. On the other hand, Beijing has been aiding them by making considerable investments into their country. In addition to that, the Han race's colonization of Uyghur has led to a lot of progress. That begs the question about what the Han race who are living there will face. They'll become refugees if they're thrown out of the country. That's another thing to consider.

The domestic affairs of another country are their own domestic affairs after all. There are certain matters beyond the power of foreign intervention.

Self-governing countries need to govern themselves. For example, let's say that a civil war or some other conflict over the election result is erupting between the Republicans and Democrats in America and therefore a foreign country that wants to take advantage of this situation sends military forces to incite confusion there. It's something that won't be forgiven after all, and the same thing goes for other countries. Yeah.

His basic way of thinking regarding defending Taiwan

B
I'd like to continue the current context of what you just said, and talk about Taiwan, then.

BIDEN'S G.S.
Aah, okay, okay, okay.

B
Because of America's transition to a Biden presidency, Taiwan is also facing an atmosphere of crisis now. They're start-

ing the count down to the day that the People's Liberation Army will make an assault on them. So I want to ask you straightforwardly: will President Biden protect Taiwan?

BIDEN'S G.S.
In reality, Tsai Ing-Wen's approval ratings have been steeply dropping now, since I won the election. Meaning that she was able to take a strong stance (against Beijing) when Trump was the president and ask him for as much military weapons aid as necessary in addition to American cooperation in joint-defense measures. But the fact that her ratings dropped as soon as I won the election shows that Taiwan could be defeated by Beijing if they maintain a strong stance against Beijing. In other words, this means we'll have to review the military arms deal that Trump and Taiwan agreed on during his presidency. Yeah.

B
Who do you mean? Who will be reviewing the arms deal: President Tsai Ing-Wen or President Biden?

BIDEN'S G.S.
America, of course.

B

In other words, the arms deals and other...

BIDEN'S G.S.

The plan was to sell military arms to them. But it's possible that we'll retract.

B

Is that so? Okay, you're already...

BIDEN'S G.S.

Because that's what will happen if pressure is put on them.

B

Oh, what you just now said will become a huge scoop today...

A

About the pressure you just referred to, which intention are you referring to, or where is the pressure being directed?

BIDEN'S G.S.

Well, Taiwan will get assimilated by China anyway.

A
Ah, I see.

BIDEN'S G.S.
If that's the case, they shouldn't carelessly let people die. They should make that transition peacefully.

A
Then, with regard to Japan, you also ...

BIDEN'S G.S.
When Ma Ying-Jeou was the president of Taiwan, didn't Taiwan make the transfer to the Beijing dialect? Yeah. And wasn't Taiwan preparing to become a Chinese province? This means that half of Taiwan is alright with that happening to themselves. But because Trump said that he will support the hardliners, the hardliners have stood up and tried to fight China. But how could such a small country like Taiwan defeat China? Taiwan has no chance against them unless America fights for them. But the mothers of America won't want to allow that. So Taiwan should just get assimilated peacefully.

B

That's a very serious statement you are making.

BIDEN'S G.S.

Oh, is it?

B

Yes. It's very, very huge.

BIDEN'S G.S.

China has a population of 1.4 billion people! In comparison, Hong Kong has only 7 million people. And it's the 20 million people of Taiwan going against the 1.4 billion people of China. Taiwan is the size of just a city. They should just join China. They should just become a province of it.

B

What you had said just now will impact the world very significantly. From now on, you'll face a lot of counter-reactions...

BIDEN'S G.S.

In order to handle that issue ... so, right now, I'm trying to implement changes to our industrial structure so that we can end our dependence on Iran and Iraq for oil. By creating industries that have no carbon emissions, we can weaken the oil-producing countries. Doing this will weaken their economic power. People say that the areas around Taiwan need to be protected in order to protect our oil tankers' sea routes. But getting rid of the need for oil altogether will mean that, well, what happens to Taiwan wouldn't matter to us anymore.

His value judgment on the battle between democracy and totalitarianism

A
Just now you brought up a little bit about Ma Ying-Jeou's presidency. Was that a sign that that kind of political movement had already started during Obama's presidency as kind of a secret agreement between America and Beijing?

BIDEN'S G.S.
Taiwan has no chance of winning, of course. Isn't that an obvious result if you compare the difference in their sizes? It's clear that Taiwan's revolt of 20 million people doesn't

have any chance of winning. The longer that such a confrontation lasts, the more deaths there will be. And since Beijing will obviously apply strong military force, Taiwan will become like Okinawa. Yeah.

B
We're trying to ask you about your value judgment on this issue. What's justice for you? What are human rights for you?

BIDEN'S G.S.
But look at Japan. Japan does nothing. Taiwan used to be a colony of Japan, you know. Japan used to be like Britain before. The UK now is agreeing to accept refugees from Hong Kong. Since Taiwan used to be a colony of Japan, why doesn't Japan at least agree to accept Taiwanese refugees if anything happens to Taiwan? Isn't that something that Japan could say?

B
Yes, that's something that Japan should consider at another time.

BIDEN'S G.S.
I bet your country has no intention to do so.

B

In other words, a battle between totalitarianism and democracy is occurring in these Taiwan-related issues. We want to know what Mr. Biden's value judgment regarding justice will be.

BIDEN'S G.S.

If you lose in a war, it wouldn't matter whether you believe that totalitarianism is justice or that democracy is justice. If you lose, it will mean the end of everything. Even though people say that World War II was democracy's victory over totalitarianism, the reality was that it was more complicated than that, as people here also know.

So, another fierce battle with the Soviets has resumed, and no one had imagined that the country they had previously saved—China, under Mao Zedong's rule—would become what it is now. It's difficult to foresee such a thing historically.

America might also face a war against totalitarianism, but look at what has happened. People thought America was a democratic country but they were very wrong. Democracy was coming to an end during Trump's four years as president. All of America's mass media think that Trump is a

"Hitler." They're saying that "Hitler" isn't in China but in America. Yeah.

Mr. Biden's guardian spirit calls Mr. Trump a "crazy person"

A
Who do you think is more dangerous, Xi Jinping or Trump?

BIDEN'S G.S.
Trump would definitely be more dangerous!

A
So that's how you see things.

BIDEN'S G.S.
That guy is really crazy, you know. In America's case, the missile will really fly if he pushes the button. I don't think that Xi Jinping would as easily be able to do that because it could sometimes lead to fall from power. With Trump, it's really possible for him to press the button. That's why right

now we should be hurrying . . . A few hours are still left. Trump escaped to Florida while still in possession of the nuclear missile button, so we have to quickly deactivate that and get a replacement. He could end up doing something before that's done. That button actually should probably be deactivated before the inaugural ceremony. But we don't conduct any meetings for handing over presidential work.

B
Well, in roughly 13 hours from now, you will switch places with Trump.

BIDEN'S G.S.
Yeah, it was a close call. If we let someone crazy rule America, it would be worse than Hitler's time. Hitler didn't have nuclear weapons, not yet.

B
Wait a moment—I want to make sure I correctly understand you. Are you saying that when you look at the situation with totalitarian characteristics in mind, you believe that Trump is more dangerous than Xi Jinping and that compared with Trump, Xi Jinping is much weaker?

BIDEN'S G.S.

Look at him. Our country is supposed to be the origin of democracy, but look at what he did when the Democrats won two congressional seats in the runoff elections; these wins gave the Democrats equal power and the upper hand, as the Speaker of the House is also a Democrat. So then he told the people—the mob—to occupy Congress. Doing something like that is just crazy. He's a total dictator.

B

The preliminary briefing for President Biden's inaugural address that was released said that he'll basically speak on the theme of unity instead of division. What you're saying right now, in this interview, is also going to be translated and released in America. And about half of the American people have voted for Trump.

BIDEN'S G.S.

Well, the approval rating for Trump was at 29 percent the other day. I think that now it's dropped even lower than that. It's probably at 20 percent, by now.

B

Okay, I saw sources that said that but also saw sources that didn't say that. Well, we sincerely ask you that if you truly want to unite America, then please consider the will of the 74 million Americans who voted for Trump. This is what presidents throughout American history have done, and doing so would be true democracy.

BIDEN'S G.S.

No, he was just the first cult president since this nation's beginning. Everyone was on the verge of getting brainwashed. That almost happened. Anyway, what I need to do right now is stop America from getting divided and help the people who are getting the coronavirus. That's my first goal of this year. As the president, I can't do something stupid like start a war in the middle of this situation. So, foreign diplomacy will need to be handled very carefully. Carefully, I'll try to indicate the direction we should head toward as I deal with our domestic problems first.

B

So you're saying that that's your main stance.

BIDEN'S G.S.

Oh, yeah, yeah. If Trump had continued as president, we would possibly have gone to war with China by February or March. If he would have sent warships over to battle Beijing simply because Beijing threatened Taiwan or Hong Kong a war would have started. The military is currently prepared for both war or peace, and now that the president will change, they're waiting for what kind of directions and words I will give them.

He believes that the Senkaku Islands issue and the Japanese constitution's revision are Japan's responsibilities

A

I would also like to ask you regarding Japan's relationship with America. During the end of the Abe administration, there was mention about Japan getting its ability to attack foreign enemy bases.

BIDEN'S G.S.
Well, you should stop talking about the things you're not able to do.

A
There's the issue about Chinese public vessels intruding into Japan's territorial waters near the Senkaku Islands.

BIDEN'S G.S.
Just hand the Senkaku Islands over to Beijing because you can't win against Beijing.

A
What are Mr. Biden's thoughts about the Japanese administration and Japan's Self-Defense Forces?

BIDEN'S G.S.
That issue is up to the Japanese people's willingness. When MacArthur told Japan that it can set up a military, it decided not to do so. Japan itself needs to take responsibility for that decision.

Japan should just set one up. If you're a democratic nation, then you should hold an election to decide what to do.

But the people aren't given the chance to vote on that issue. And if you hold an election on that issue, the minority party is definitely going to win the votes, which is what the people of Japan are supporting.

No one is living in the Senkaku Islands. If Beijing takes control of it, they might put up China's flag, live there, and build a military base there, like they did in the Nansa Islands. But you wouldn't be able to do anything anyway. That's Japan's responsibility, not America's.

A
In that case, you're at least not against Japan revising the constitution?

BIDEN'S G.S.
Do it yourselves. You're a self-governing country. We don't care what happens to a tiny country like Japan. You might have 120 million people living in a country as tiny in size as California, but I don't care if you end up having to escape to Australia or about whatever you have to do. As America's president, I have nothing to do with that.

B

Okay, we now understand what you're really thinking.

BIDEN'S G.S.

We were also originally a colony. We were also like Uyghur, I'll tell you that. I'm starting to get really angry, so I'll tell you that.

6

Asking Biden's Guardian Spirit about His Vision of the World

On his stance on Iran–Israel issues

B

Okay. There's one more topic left. Master Ryuho Okawa of Happy Science views the world from the eyes of a World Teacher.

BIDEN'S G.S.

I haven't heard of that.

B

With that perspective in mind, I have a question to ask you for the sake of the people around the world. The whole world is holding their breaths and watching what kind of stance Biden's administration will take with Iran. What is his administration planning to do?

BIDEN'S G.S.

Well, I'm sure Iran must be thrilled right now.

How President Biden Will Deal with Critical Global Issues

B

Well, if you make even the slightest false move, we could find ourselves in a dangerous situation because Israel could possibly get involved. This is what everyone is worried about. Have you been repeatedly postponing decisions on this issue or trying to avoid making a decision? Or are you planning to simply revert back to what the Obama presidency did? What are you intending to do about this issue? Actually, everyone is watching what you will do very closely. Could you tell us your plan?

BIDEN'S G.S.

Iran is thanking me. Iran is grateful right now because thanks to Allah, Trump got defeated. Toward you, Iran's attitude is really... how should I say this, they're actually supporting... they must be thinking, "We were right. When we developed a connection with Happy Science [*claps his hand twice*], Allah sided with us and Trump got defeated. And right now Israel's dictator is squirming, but we're sure that he'll also eventually get wiped out."

Who was it? Trump's daughter and her husband? Because of their belief in Judaism, Israel has been doing anything it wants to do. Now it'll be destroyed, and peace will come to the Arab world. Everything is now going to get better.

B

Many people are worried that if that happens, there's no doubt that Prime Minister Netanyahu of Israel will act aggressively on his own will.

BIDEN'S G.S.

Well, we have to kill Netanyahu. He's a Hitler. Even though he's also small.

B

Well, what you just now said will become the American President's words. So, it's a little [*smiles wryly*] …

BIDEN'S G.S.

We need to crush him because we also want to destroy Trump from the roots.

B

We now understand that that's what is really going through Biden's mind. But everyone is worried that if President Biden really decides to side with Iran, then Israel, who is armed with many kinds of weapons, could act aggressively on its own will. And in that case, there's the risk of a limited nuclear war or some kind of conflict erupting.

BIDEN'S G.S.
Well, those weapons are mostly coming from the US anyway, similar to how it is in Taiwan. America just has to stop supplying them to Israel, which will cut off Israel's ability to continue fighting. They'll run out of weapons in no time.

B
Okay, is this what you're saying then: if you side with Iran, then Israel might take aggressive action, but you have no idea what you'll do if this happens?

BIDEN'S G.S.
That's an issue that the Arabs should discuss among themselves. I have nothing to do with it.

B
You "have nothing to do with it"?

BIDEN'S G.S.
They're always fighting there. I have nothing to do with them.

C
Well, if that happens, and if the situation in the Middle East gets very bad ...

BIDEN'S G.S.
Ah, yeah, there's no justice on either of the sides, regardless of how you look at it.

C
You're not going to send over American forces?

BIDEN'S G.S.
Hm?

C
When the Middle East falls into chaos and war erupts, you're not going to send the American military?

BIDEN'S G.S.
Europe is much closer to the Middle East, so Europe should decide what to do about that issue. The EU should decide about that.

B

Okay, so your stance is that Europe should decide what to do.

BIDEN'S G.S.

Yeah, the EU should decide what to do. They should determine what is more beneficial—protecting Israel, the land of their ancestral souls, or protecting the oil-producing countries. Greta is a hero in light of this issue. If the world can operate without oil, those countries wouldn't have anything to trouble the world.

B

Okay, so you want to tell Europe to decide, by itself, about how to deal with the Iran-Israel issue, and that America has nothing to do with this issue?

BIDEN'S G.S.

Europe should decide.

B

I see.

BIDEN'S G.S.
And then the US will decide whether to agree with the decision or not, I guess.

He warns that Japan should fear more about Russia's possible assault on Hokkaido

C
In that case, with regard to the Japan–US alliance, are you going to tell Japan that it should do what it can do on its own?

BIDEN'S G.S.
Well, the Japan–US alliance is like the thin ice of an early spring lake. Skating on top of it may feel enjoyable, but who knows what might happen in the future.

C
There's talk of President Biden possibly taking a tough stance against Russia.

BIDEN'S G.S.
Yeah I'm very sure that he will. Russia is dangerous. They're dangerous. Yeah.

C
If that happens, then China and Russia could join forces against America and also try to lure Japan into joining them from thinking that America is weakening now.

BIDEN'S G.S.
You should fear more about Hokkaido being taken over. China will come to take the Senkaku Islands and Okinawa from you, and then Russia will be the next to make a move on you. Because of decades of nagging by Japan and the conning scheme to retake the Four Northern Islands from Russia, Russia will come to take Hokkaido from you. Russia has been deeply wanting to do so.

During World War II, the Soviets fought Hitler in the Russo-German war, and suffered a huge number of deaths, nearly numbering... I think it was about 20 million fatalities. They joined the winning Allied powers at this cost to themselves and continued to battle until Berlin's fall. Yet the Soviets didn't receive much in return for that. There's a lot of built-up frustration inside them because of this. The Soviets—current Russia—demanded half of Japan, the eastern half of Japan, but they only got the Four Northern Islands instead. Despite that this is what happened, Japan is continuing to demand the return of the Four Northern Islands.

I wouldn't blame Russia for wanting to bomb a cheapskate country like yours. I think so. So be careful not to show them any signs of weakness. Thinking only about your defense against China could mean suddenly losing Hokkaido to Russia. Because your attention has been drawn toward China, your PAC-3's locations have moved closer to China now, leaving Hokkaido completely open to attack.

A
That's a very novel opinion to have as America's president.

BIDEN'S G.S.
Isn't it very novel? It's outrageous to think that I could be going senile. How could they say such a thing about me? It's the complete opposite of that. I have very progressive thinking.

If China grows, he'll extract
as much money from it as he can

A

Have you thought about what your vision of the world would be? For example, have you thought of dividing the world between America and China? Are there any ideas you have about the direction you want to head in, or a vision of what you want to do with the world?

BIDEN'S G.S.

Well, I have no intention of going to war with China. However, if China grows, which is very possible because of its huge population, and it keeps progressing at the current rate, then I want to extract as much of its wealth as I can. I'll develop a system that will extract its wealth and use that as power to support declining areas of America. So, since China will probably become a major power of the world, I don't see why we shouldn't let China rule Asia. Yeah. It's not that we are interested in Asia.

B

Basically, all that you've said, including what you've just told us, is almost the same as what Mr. Obama's guardian spirit talked about when Mr. Obama was inaugurated into office. The contents have all been the same.

BIDEN'S G.S.

Well, that's probably true. Yeah.

B

It's making us feel that things will go backward in time and we will repeat the same things over again.

BIDEN'S G.S.

Well, Trump was . . . the mistake in your level of awareness, your enlightenment, is that your Master didn't realize that Trump was the second coming of Hitler. You have to repent about that! Your support for Trump led you to the downfall you're facing now. If you raise me up and say that Biden must be God . . . can't you tell by talking with me that I'm greater than Shakyamuni Buddha and Jesus Christ?

He mentions that a peculiar person is the determiner of America's justice

A
Okay, well, we've discussed various things with you now. And we'd like to start rounding up this interview. The other day, a spirit who came to Happy Science informed us about some things. For example, we heard that as soon as Xi Jinping came to power, he came under the influence of a walk-in by something.

BIDEN'S G.S.
Oh, really?

A
When you reach a certain level of position, there are guiding spirits and other kinds of spiritual powers that could start influencing you. Do you sense any kind of spiritual being that could be guiding you or that could have started to do so?

BIDEN'S G.S.
That would be my wife.

A
Who?

BIDEN'S G.S.
I'm the most afraid of my wife.

A
My question wasn't meant in an earthly sense.

BIDEN'S G.S.
My answer was in an earthly sense. She is the scariest. I'm not afraid of spiritual beings. She's very scary. She's a teacher, so she's very stern. Yeah. My wife will determine what justice is.

A
Okay... [*laughs wryly*].

B
Oh, really.

BIDEN'S G.S.
The same thing is happening right here.

B
No, no, no.

BIDEN'S G.S.
When I came to Happy Science the other night, I heard her saying "There's no way we'll let President Biden give a spiritual interview!" And I was blocked out outright. So I came back requesting a rematch. And here I am today.

B
That's besides the issue we're talking about. As the president of America, who possesses the strongest power in the world, are you saying that America's justice will be determined by Mr. Biden's wife?

BIDEN'S G.S.
Yes, she's the First Lady. Of course, the First Lady is going to.

B
[*Laughs wryly*] Is that really so . . .?

BIDEN'S G.S.
Isn't it the same with Trump? I'm sure that his decisions are coming from the weak brain of that tall, former fashion model.

He says that the president of America has enough power to destroy the planet

A
According to Happy Science's spiritual research, Mr. Trump was George Washington in a past life.

BIDEN'S G.S.
George Washington was a farmer when America was a small, weak country. Guerilla warfare ...

A
And in your last spiritual interview that was published ...

BIDEN'S G.S.
I was like an exemplar model of a law-based government.

How President Biden Will Deal with Critical Global Issues

A
... you revealed that you were just a sheriff.

BIDEN'S G.S.
Yeah, I was a role model of law-based government during a time when America was changing into a law-based nation. Yeah ...

A
I'm sure that the president of America bears a much larger mission than a sheriff does.

BIDEN'S G.S.
Ah, well he (Mr. Trump) was the boss of "guerilla forces." That's what he was. "Guerilla wars" were what he was fighting.

A
What is your understanding of the spirit world?

BIDEN'S G.S.
I don't know anything about it.

A
Have you spoken with anyone?

BIDEN'S G.S.
I don't know what you're talking about. But the position of the president of America is greater than that of the ancient pharaohs of Egypt, and the president has the power to destroy the Earth. So you could be telling people that an evil space being named Ahriman has come from the universe. I don't know whether you're lying or not, but even if this were true, I'm stronger than Ahriman. I have the power to destroy all countries other than America. Well, at least that power will be mine in a few more hours.

As soon as I get inaugurated and it's clear that I'm free of mental insanity issues, I could order us to "Launch the missile!" and completely destroy Europe, Japan, China, or anyone else. The coronavirus isn't even an issue. If I become really serious, China won't exist in several hours from now. That's what having supreme power means, and this is the reason you're supposed to give others a break.

What he thinks of
Kamala Harris and Hillary Clinton

B
Ummm...

BIDEN'S G.S.
Did I make you speechless?

B
No, that's not the case at all...

BIDEN'S G.S.
Pay your "devotion" to me.

B
Could I ask you one thing? Summarizing in a few words everything you just spoke to us about, if you will do everything just as you told us today, then America will face many kinds of crises in roughly a year from now...

BIDEN'S G.S.
Oh, really?

B

Yes. Objectively speaking, we can predict that crises will come in the areas of economics, foreign diplomacy, and elsewhere.

BIDEN'S G.S.

Hmmm.

B

Noticing that fact, I'm very sorry to have to ask you this question. But since you have had health problems...

BIDEN'S G.S.

Ah.

B

So my question is about the incumbent vice president, Ms. Kamala Harris.

BIDEN'S G.S.

Uhuh. Uhuh. Uhuh. Uhuh.

B

What kind of person do you think she is, and what do you think of her?

BIDEN'S G.S.

Well, she was just a way to get more votes.

B

That is your reason for choosing her?

BIDEN'S G.S.

Yeah, because I don't think she actually likes me that much, either. And I don't like her either. I don't like her, but by choosing her, I would be able to gather votes from women, Black people, and other colored people, like Yellow people. She also has some Indian ancestry in her, so that would foster a good relationship with India. Those things are what we thought about when choosing her. So yeah, I basically chose her for more votes.

B

Okay. If that's the case, then have you considered what would happen if you need to give your position to her . . . ?

BIDEN'S G.S.
Give my position to her?

B
Yes, because it's possible that she will have to take your place; in other words...

BIDEN'S G.S.
Wait one second, mister, that's...

B
I'm asking you just in case. As long as that could be seen as a possibility, part of your responsibility when appointing her was to consider that possibility. What have you considered about her with regard to this issue?

BIDEN'S G.S.
Hmmm.

B
In other words, what do you think of her capability?

BIDEN'S G.S.

Well, if that were to happen within my four-year term . . . the next election would be very near. Is Trump thinking of running in that election? I'll destroy his willpower by completely destroying all of his lines of business. That's what I'm thinking of doing.

B

Wait. But that's a very . . . that's a shocking thing to hear.

BIDEN'S G.S.

I'll make him "America's Number One King of Debts." That's what I want to do with him. I'm capable of destroying him, so that's what I'm going to do. All of Trump's businesses; his daughter's and her husband's too. There's her fashion line and his real estate business. I'll drive all of their businesses to the point that they're forced to sell their Trump Tower vacation home. Doing that would force Trump to defect to another country. Yeah. Yeah. So I'm going to make sure he won't be running in the next election.

B
Then, in that case, your reason for appointing Ms. Harris wasn't that you believed she had good character, views, and ability?

BIDEN'S G.S.
Well, I'm definitely going to destroy Trump. But if a good Republican candidate other than him appears, I think that they can run against each other.

But sometimes it's actually better to not have ability. She (Kamala Harris) wouldn't be capable of doing this. . . . But Hillary received more votes than Trump did in the previous election four years ago, and had she been the one elected president, she would have attacked China by now. She would have already done so—I think so. It's not true that the Democrats don't wage wars. That completely depends on the person. Based on how Hillary tends to think, she would have attacked China. So Trump's willpower is weaker. To minimize costs as much as possible and avoid facing criticism, he likes to assassinate individual people, but Hillary would've waged a war. If Hillary had become the president, we would be fighting a war somewhere in southern China now. In that sense, it was a good thing that she didn't become the president, but I believe that I became the president to stop Trump from starting the war. I don't know about Kamala, but when it comes to Americans, I'm sure that Americans will handle it intelligently. I'm sure of that. Yeah.

He foresees competition between GAFA

C
Just now I sensed that you're also going to suppress other Republicans, and in that case . . .

BIDEN'S G.S.
By saying "others," . . . well, what I said was that I'll destroy Trump, but if other good candidates appear, then the American people should make the decision. Yeah.

C
I see. An issue that received a lot of attention this time was the Big Tech: GAFA.

BIDEN'S G.S.
Uhuh. Uhuh. Uhuh.

C
Twitter shut down President Trump's account.

BIDEN'S G.S.
Uhuh. Uhuh. Uhuh.

C
This is a big issue that the conservatives are talking about.

BIDEN'S G.S.
Well, it must mean that many supporters of me are everywhere.

C
But actions like those of GAFA could lead to creating an IT-controlled, digital totalitarian system, and I'd like to ask you what President Biden thinks about this issue.

BIDEN'S G.S.
I don't know anything about it. Nothing at all. Each of the GAFA companies is like an additional state to the 50 united states to me, I guess.

C
So, if they support you, you're going to leave them alone?

BIDEN'S G.S.
Well, competition will remain among them. So I don't think all of them will survive. So instead of the government taking action on them, they'll try to destroy each other anyway. Probably two of them will survive at the end. Probably two of them will get defeated.

In other words, it's possible to control them by letting them compete with each other. I think that doing this will be enough and better than getting government regulation involved. It was good of them to "cut off Trump's head." By doing that, they contributed to establishing a government of good. But I don't know what will happen from here on.

7

What Will Biden's Presidency Bring to America?

Biden's guardian spirit appears to be full of energy at this time, unlike during the last spiritual interview

A

I think you've spoken with us now about many of your views on the domestic affairs of America and also on foreign diplomacy. I'm just wondering about when you came here a week ago. You, Mr. Biden's guardian spirit, were in a state of great distress at that time and mentally, your spirits were low when you came back in November. But you seem to be in good spirits today.

BIDEN'S G.S.

Well, that's because I was in danger of getting assassinated by midnight tonight. And look at what Trump did. He literally gave a speech where he'll be visible to Congress. Then, afterward, the hundreds or thousands of people who listened rolled into the highly secure Capitol building. Someone broke the window and came in.

That is scary. He is violent. He might be the real reincarnation of the guy at the guillotine during the French Revolution. You should redo your spiritual research on him. You could have been wrong about his past life as George Washington. He's probably the person who beheaded many people during the French Revolution.

A
Does Mr. Biden feel more power inside himself, more than before?

BIDEN'S G.S.
Aah, yeah, he can feel himself filled with the delight of the 300 million people who support him and believe that he's going to be their savior.

A
Where is that energy coming from? We want to know.

BIDEN'S G.S.

Well, he hasn't made a mistake yet, you know, although he might make some going forward now [*laughs*]. But at least he'll get to start with a perfect score.

A

You mentioned Ahriman a moment ago.

BIDEN'S G.S.

Yeah, I mentioned his name because I happened to overhear about him.

A

Do you ever sense any evil presences near you?

BIDEN'S G.S.

You're going to say that Ahriman is influencing Beijing or something like that, aren't you? But I'm capable of destroying China itself, so I'm not afraid of any evil-doing being inside of Beijing. Yeah. I'm not afraid of something like that at all.

China [*speaking as he pounds the desk*] could have 400 rounds of nuclear weapons, but in comparison with that,

America is capable of finishing them off in one day if we decide to get serious.

Biden's guardian spirit feels like Lincoln when he won the Civil War

A
I know I'm being persistent, but are there any spiritual beings around you, such as guiding spirits or friends who are giving you advice? Have you noticed anyone like that around you?

BIDEN'S G.S.
Well, my feelings right now are like Lincoln's. Yeah. Yeah. I have the same feelings as Lincoln did. Mhm. Lincoln. The feelings of Lincoln when he won the Civil War. Those are my feelings right now. Trump tried to start a civil war, and he was on the side of the Confederates.

A
Are there any beings around you who are advising you or any military commanders or military advisors who are helping you?

BIDEN'S G.S.

Your words sound so much like Latin to me that I can't understand what you're asking me. Tell me what you're trying to say.

A

Do you have any friends near you?

BIDEN'S G.S.

Please, in easy Japanese or in easy English: what do you want to know?

A

Anyone who you're close with?

BIDEN'S G.S.

Who are you referring to as "friends"? The president isn't allowed to have friends.

A

Is there anyone you're close with?

How President Biden Will Deal with Critical Global Issues

BIDEN'S G.S.

I'm not supposed to have someone like that near me. Presidents need to make decisions alone. Yeah.

A

Is there anyone who you talk to when you're in trouble?

BIDEN'S G.S.

Didn't I tell you already that my wife makes the final decisions? What are you trying to ask me? Go ask my wife that kind of question.

A

Okay, I got a good sense of things now.

BIDEN'S G.S.

The president of France also does that, you know. Yeah. He also follows all of his wife's decisions. This is the age of women now. Yeah.

A

Are you aware that there is a God?

BIDEN'S G.S.

Who? God? Yeah, God is somewhere. I'm sure that he exists. God supported me fairly. So, this book that says, "God chose Trump to be president-elect!" must be referring to Israel's god. Probably. This god is probably Israel's god who was supporting Trump to help Netanyahu. So it must have been the ethnic god of Israel who said such a thing. That's what you should think. The God of America is different now. He's the God of the world now. Yeah. Mhm.

A

Meaning you feel as if you've become the God of America?

His value judgment is that he'll always take the side of the larger population and higher G.D.P.

BIDEN'S G.S.

Well, I feel I'm getting close to Godhood, after all. I'm near that—I think so. It's a really nice feeling to become the president. You should also experience this feeling some time, yeah. It's a really good feeling. Mhm. Try getting 8 million people to vote for you. You also have a political party, don't you? Well, one that's only in name. You're not getting any votes, right? The power of getting 8 million votes is a really good feeling.

A
Okay, I've gained some understanding of what you're thinking.

BIDEN'S G.S.
As a human being, you first have to be righteous. You have to have a nice personality. You need a high level of awareness as a human being. Yeah.

A
Well, your way of determining righteousness has not been clear.

BIDEN'S G.S.
Yeah, well, I was weak-spirited before because I intruded into your Master's bedroom. I felt very apologetic for doing so, and I became very fearful of his wife's power. That's the only reason I acted weak-spiritedly. But I can talk this way with male interviewers during the daytime. That's what I'm saying. Yeah.

A

Okay, were you able to tell us your thoughts confidently today then?

BIDEN'S G.S.

Yeah. So, [*pointing to interviewer B*] your magazine[6] is going to get stopped very soon. And you, [*pointing to interviewer A*] your International Politics Division will get closed down soon. And you, [*pointing to interviewer C*] you should get a profit-making job somewhere else again. Okay? And that'll be the end. Yeah.

B

Actually, thanks to the news about Biden's scandal coming out, we've seen growth in sales—the web edition included. We are very thankful for that success and are working hard toward our further growth.

BIDEN'S G.S.

Your fake news has got to get defeated. The fakes have to get destroyed. The fake news you're spreading to the Japanese people is deceiving them. It's the Biden-backing major newspapers who were right after all. When all is said and done, CNN was the news media truly representing the world. Yeah.

A
Well, I see that it is really time to seriously think about what world justice is.

BIDEN'S G.S.
I've already told you this clearly, but my decisions will be based on the size of the population and the G.D.P. As long as you know that, you'll understand my actions. Yes. Meaning I'll always side with the bigger side. Yes.

A
We understand that. Thank you very much for speaking with us today.

He believes that information about space beings should just be handled by NASA

BIDEN'S G.S.
Was that okay? Was that really enough for you? Was it enough? Does anyone else have a question? The people here going out of business don't want to ask me anything else? Are you sure? Is it okay?

C
I have just one question then. Will you be taking over the classified information about space beings?

BIDEN'S G.S.
Ahh ... It's not an area that I'm interested in. I get reports on that, but I'm not going to have any work from Trump passed on to me. Somewhere ... (Actually, before leaving the official residence, Mr. Trump left instructions to release information on UFOs and space beings.) But, well, everyone in government positions will also get replaced, so I don't know if any information like that will get released or not. Yeah. I don't have any information about space beings even if you asked me.

That's something that NASA can do about as they want. Why should I care about that? The job of a president is to watch things from a broad perspective. Yeah.

So, it's all good. The world's been saved now. Under Trump's dictatorship ... Trump wanted to work hard by himself only on strange details but not on anything he wasn't interested in. Now that a fussy president like him is gone, the world will become a better place, just like when the rain clouds clear away to reveal blue skies. Yeah.

Somehow, I feel a lot of power inside of me today. Maybe it's coming from the thoughts of congratulations from the American people. It feels like the whole world is celebrating for me.

Whether Mr. Suga gets crushed or he survives, it all depends on me, you know? I can choose either of those outcomes. Yeah.

A
Okay. Thank you very much for being very frank and honest in today's interview with us.

BIDEN'S G.S.
Yeah. Yeah. Mr. Suga wants to visit America, but well, everything will get decided by whether or not I propose to give him aid. If I abandon him, then that would be the end of his term, you know. Yeah. His term could end as soon as the beginning of spring. You know? But if I play a card, then his term might last a little longer. Well, that's all. Yeah.

A
The things you spoke with us about today will become valuable information for us.

He says that Happy Science will survive if they praise him

BIDEN'S G.S.
Yeah. Well, your status will probably rise because of this interview with me. But because it will just be an empty status, you should think you'll eventually lose them. Okay? [*Speaking to interviewer B*] Your magazine should just get acquired by *Shukan Shicho*. Yeah.

B
We've already seen our sales figures make a turnaround, so that won't be necessary. We'll keep doing our best.

A
Yes. Thank you very much.

BIDEN'S G.S.
Hmm, did I really complete my mission? [*Pointing to the book titled* Spiritual Interviews with the Guardian Spirits of Biden and Trump] Look at how unfair you've been. Why would you show a bigger picture of the defeated guy and a smaller picture of the guy getting elected in the future? You

were already making a mistake when you made this decision. This is why IRH Press is going to go out of business this year. Yeah.

B
I think that now we've gained a good overall understanding of what's inside your mind and what kind of things we should expect to happen over the course of a year or so . . .

BIDEN'S G.S.
You understand now?

B
Yes. Because we have a general idea now, we can also start thinking about our strategy.

BIDEN'S G.S.
All you need to do is keep praising me, and by doing that, you'll be able to survive. It's as easy as that. Or else, watch out! You won't be able to spread the Truths in America! If you want to get involved with America's president, you need millions of believers in America. Yeah. Otherwise, this is just ridiculous.

B

No matter what you say to us, we clearly saw that tens of millions of Americans are thinking and feeling the same way we are. Either way, America is a land of religious freedom, so we're going to work hard there.

BIDEN'S G.S.

I'll probably be fine until the inauguration ceremony . . . Hmmm. Well, actually, some Republicans from the military and the police departments have participated in the demonstrations. We're investigating these people as we speak. National Guardsmen are staying in Capitol Hill overnight, and some of them could be extreme Republican conservatives. As we speak, we're doing our best to investigate into them for several more hours. We'll need to remove the dangerous ones, as it's possible that someone could revolt from the inside. . . . In other words, we can't let a revolt actually happen from within when we expect one to happen from the outside. So, we're in the middle of thoroughly investigating them. I hope we can get through these several hours somehow. Yeah.

A
Thank you very much for telling us everything including your current state of mind so we can easily understand it.

BIDEN'S G.S.
If you aren't a little nicer to the Democratic Party, you might not be able to do missionary work in America. You might get stopped from entering the country, you know. Soon you might get banned from entering, mister.

A
America is a free country.

BIDEN'S G.S.
You might get banned from entering America if you don't discontinue your books on Trump. You'll become a wanted criminal soon, you know.

A
No, no. I also have many close friends in America, actually.

B
We're essentially a religion. Our goal is to save all of humankind.

BIDEN'S G.S.
Hmmm.

A
We want to spread the Truths to everyone, including members of the Democratic Party.

BIDEN'S G.S.
Hmmm.

B
So you don't have to worry about that, I assure you.

BIDEN'S G.S.
Actually, all of you . . . if you keep going at the same rate that you are, it will become impossible for you to succeed in Hollywood. The people of Hollywood are supporting the leftists because they want the market of 1.4 billion Chinese people. Stop trying to get in their way, okay? You're not supposed to get in their way.

A
Thank you very much for talking with us about your very "unique" views.

BIDEN'S G.S.
It's been a while since the last time I gave a unique opinion! It's very painful when you don't get to speak your views.

A
We could get a good sense of your personality.

BIDEN'S G.S.
It feels good to be on top of the world. There's no one above you. No one—I see only blue skies above me.

A
This interview will become a big scoop in both America and Japan. We're very thankful you could give us the valuable chance to talk with you.

Will the world go in the righteous direction under President Biden?

BIDEN'S G.S.
Since all of these men were weak, are there any strong women here? I'll take questions if anyone wants to ask one.

No one has a question? My personality is very kind to women. Does anyone want to ask me anything? Maybe if Mrs. D doesn't want a conclusion different from that of last time, would you like to add something...?

D
I clearly see how you will become the symbol of America's downfall.

BIDEN'S G.S.
That's not true! How could you say that [*laughs*]? I've been saying that someone like Trump who has affairs with women shouldn't become the president. Faithfulness is a basic part of human beings and a characteristic of men. So, the world is going to head in a righteous direction from now on. Yeah.

"Downfall"? Why would America get ruined? Isn't America going to succeed thanks to me?

A
I don't think that the world is necessarily going to head in the direction that you hope it will, in reality.

BIDEN'S G.S.
How will that happen?

A
Contrary to your expectations, it's possible you'll trigger America's downfall.

BIDEN'S G.S.
Why would I lead America to its downfall? Why would it get ruined when I am trying to prevent a crisis from happening? Why would America get ruined?

A
Since you want to do everything that's the opposite of what Mr. Trump did—that's what that means at least.

BIDEN'S G.S.
Yes, that's true. That's exactly true. Trump is leaving behind a lot of homework, as if to say, "Do this and do that." I'm going to repeal all of them though. I'll probably be extremely busy tomorrow from having to sign a lot of papers. Yeah.

A
We were able to thoroughly hear about what's inside your mind. Thank you very much for your advice or rather the information you gave us.

BIDEN'S G.S.
Okay. Then, well, that's all.

8

On President Biden's Character That We Saw in This Spiritual Interview

RYUHO OKAWA

[*Claps his hands twice*] Thank you. From listening to him, we could at least see that he is in a much better mood today. Well, that's fine, I think. But I could see that he doesn't really understand the economy. I could definitely see that he doesn't understand economics and management. In addition to that, even though he's known to be an expert in foreign diplomacy, I could clearly see that he doesn't have a strategy regarding war. We saw that he just thinks very simply in terms of larger versus smaller. Other than that, I saw that he's essentially a populist politician, meaning that he determines what he says based on getting newspapers and other people to say positive things about him.

On the other hand, Mr. Trump had a strong will to do what he wants to do, regardless of how badly the mass media talk about him. Maybe he became like a religious leader drawing fanatical, ardent supporters among the American people because of this.

Well, it will be interesting to see what's going to happen. But first, we'll see the results of whether masks and vaccines will significantly decrease the spread of infections and deaths in America in the next six months. So he could probably somewhat maintain his approval ratings at that point if things improve in that way. But, since I think that China will start to take action while he is working on the domestic affairs of America, the spark of war could get larger if his responses lag behind them.

Basically, since he's not taking Japan seriously, Japan will need to take essential action by itself regarding its own matters. The Happiness Realization Party really wishes we could win seats in the Diet, but if we can't, we'll at least need to make the effort to spread righteous ideas. Otherwise, if we believe everything we hear from the Japanese mass media who only copies the American media, then the country of Japan itself could become a weak country in just a moment's notice.

But overall, he didn't have in himself any sense of justice. There's no notion of justice in him, so he'll take the side that's larger in numbers. He also believes that he can win victories by not fussing about matters. In conclusion, I think that he is a populist politician.

How President Biden Will Deal with Critical Global Issues

Since America's presidents get a 100-day "honeymoon" period, no one will speak harshly about him through the months of February, March, and April.

I'd also like us to treat the Democratic Party fairly, as much as possible.

That will be all for today.

A
Yes. Thank you very much.

ENDNOTES

1, 3, 4 See Ryuho Okawa, *Spiritual Interviews with the Guardian Spirits of Biden and Trump* (Tokyo: HS Press, 2020).

2 See Chapter One of this book.

5 At the time this spiritual interview was held.

6 He is referring to *The Liberty*, a magazine printed by Happy Science Group covering opinions on economics, politics, management principles, and more. See the English web edition at *eng.the-liberty.com*.

Afterword

I believe that Mr. Biden is a weak man. He can empathize with the weak because of this, and by his mild exterior coating, he gathered people's popularity. But because he is only an ordinary man, the voice of God cannot reach him.

Contrary to that, Mr. Trump is a man of strong willpower. The voice of God is, indeed, reaching him. For the sake of the American people upon the sinking mud boat, a raft of salvation he shall build by his own efforts.

It is the beginning of the downfall of the United States of America, like the Roman Empire of the past.

O Japan, as the land of the bushido spirit (samurai spirit) you shall rise again. O before the world returns to the dark ages again, the new sun shall be made to rise by you. This is my earnest desire.

Ryuho Okawa
Master and CEO of Happy Science Group
January 29, 2021

ABOUT THE AUTHOR

RYUHO OKAWA was born on July 7th, 1956, in Tokushima, Japan. After graduating from the University of Tokyo with a law degree, he joined a Tokyo-based trading house. While working at its New York headquarters, he studied international finance at the Graduate Center of the City University of New York. In 1981, he attained Great Enlightenment and became aware that he is El Cantare with a mission to bring salvation to all humankind. In 1986, he established Happy Science. It now has members in over 140 countries across the world, with more than 700 local branches and temples as well as 10,000 missionary houses around the world. The total number of lectures has exceeded 3,250 (of which more than 150 are in English) and over 2,800 books (of which more than 550 are Spiritual Interview Series) have been published, many of which are translated into 31 languages. Many of the books, including *The Laws of the Sun* have become best sellers or million sellers. To date, Happy Science has produced 23 movies. The original story and original concept were given by the Executive Producer Ryuho Okawa. Recent movie titles are *Beautiful Lure-A Modern Tale of "Painted Skin"* (live-action movie scheduled to be released in May 2021), *Yume Handan soshite Kyoufu Taiken e* (literally, "The Interpretation of Dreams and Fearful Experience," live-action movie scheduled to be released in Summer of 2021), and *Uchu no Ho - Elohim hen -* (literally, "The Laws of the Universe - The Age of Elohim," animation movie scheduled to be released in Fall of 2021). He has also composed the lyrics and music of over 250 songs, such as theme songs and featured songs of movies. Moreover, he is the Founder of Happy Science University and Happy Science Academy (Junior and Senior High School), Founder and President of the Happiness Realization Party, Founder and Honorary Headmaster of Happy Science Institute of Government and Management, Founder of IRH Press Co., Ltd., and the Chairperson of New Star Production Co., Ltd. and ARI Production Co., Ltd.

WHAT IS EL CANTARE?

El Cantare means "the Light of the Earth," and is the Supreme God of the Earth who has been guiding humankind since the beginning of Genesis. He is whom Jesus called Father and Muhammad called Allah. Different parts of El Cantare's core consciousness have descended to Earth in the past, once as Alpha and another as Elohim. His branch spirits, such as Shakyamuni Buddha and Hermes, have descended to Earth many times and helped to flourish many civilizations. To unite various religions and to integrate various fields of study in order to build a new civilization on Earth, a part of the core consciousness has descended to Earth as Master Ryuho Okawa.

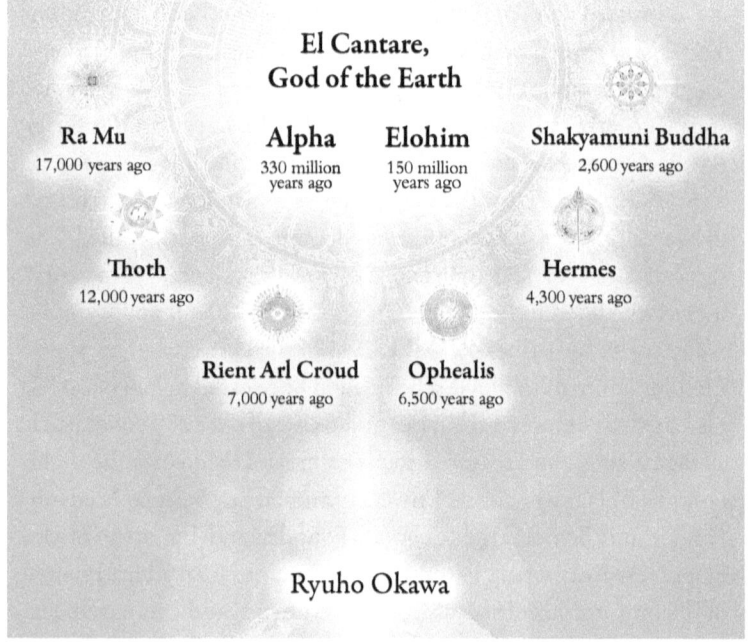

El Cantare, God of the Earth

Ra Mu — 17,000 years ago
Alpha — 330 million years ago
Elohim — 150 million years ago
Shakyamuni Buddha — 2,600 years ago

Thoth — 12,000 years ago
Hermes — 4,300 years ago

Rient Arl Croud — 7,000 years ago
Ophealis — 6,500 years ago

Ryuho Okawa

Alpha is a part of the core consciousness of El Cantare who descended to Earth around 330 million years ago. Alpha preached Earth's Truths to harmonize and unify Earth-born humans and space people who came from other planets.

Elohim is a part of El Cantare's core consciousness who descended to Earth around 150 million years ago. He gave wisdom, mainly on the differences of light and darkness, good and evil.

Shakyamuni Buddha was born as a prince into the Shakya Clan in India around 2,600 years ago. When he was 29 years old, he renounced the world and sought enlightenment. He later attained Great Enlightenment and founded Buddhism.

Hermes is one of the 12 Olympian gods in Greek mythology, but the spiritual Truth is that he taught the teachings of love and progress around 4,300 years ago that became the origin of the current Western civilization. He is a hero that truly existed.

Ophealis was born in Greece around 6,500 years ago and was the leader who took an expedition to as far as Egypt. He is the God of miracles, prosperity, and arts, and is known as Osiris in the Egyptian mythology.

Rient Arl Croud was born as a king of the ancient Incan Empire around 7,000 years ago and taught about the mysteries of the mind. In the heavenly world, he is responsible for the interactions that take place between various planets.

Thoth was an almighty leader who built the golden age of the Atlantic civilization around 12,000 years ago. In the Egyptian mythology, he is known as god Thoth.

Ra Mu was a leader who built the golden age of the civilization of Mu around 17,000 years ago. As a religious leader and a politician, he ruled by uniting religion and politics.

WHAT IS A SPIRITUAL MESSAGE?

We are all spiritual beings living on this earth. The following is the mechanism behind Master Ryuho Okawa's spiritual messages.

1 You are a spirit

People are born into this world to gain wisdom through various experiences and return to the other world when their lives end. We are all spirits and repeat this cycle in order to refine our souls.

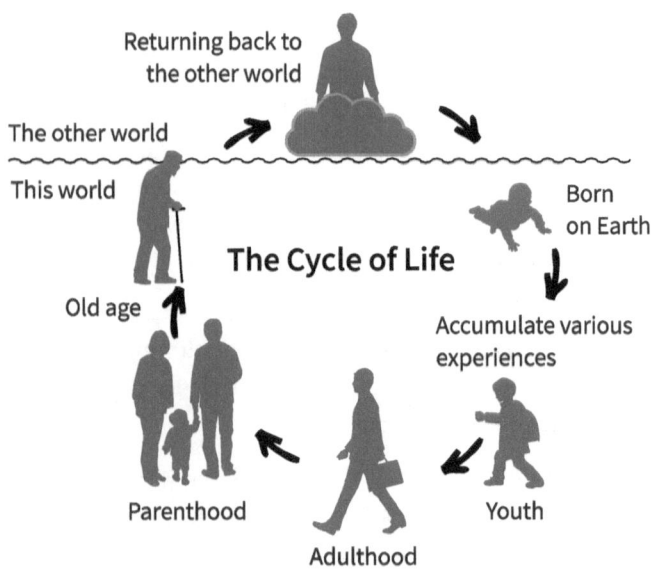

2 You have a guardian spirit

Guardian spirits are those who protect the people who are living on this earth. Each of us has a guardian spirit that watches over us and guides us from the other world. They were us in our past life, and are identical in how we think.

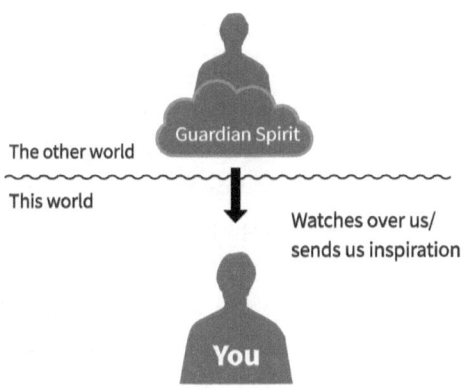

3 How spiritual messages work

Master Ryuho Okawa, through his enlightenment, is capable of summoning any spirit from anywhere in the world, including the spirit world.

Master Okawa's way of receiving spiritual messages is fundamentally different from that of other psychic mediums who undergo trances and are thereby completely taken over by the spirits they are channeling.

Master Okawa's attainment of a high level of enlightenment enables him to retain full control of his consciousness and body throughout the duration of the spiritual message. To allow the spirits to express their own thoughts and personalities freely, however, Master Okawa usually softens the dominancy of his consciousness. This way, he is able to keep his own philosophies out of the way and ensure that the spiritual messages are pure expressions of the spirits he is channeling.

Since guardian spirits think at the same subconscious level as the person living on earth, Master Okawa can summon the spirit and find out what the person on earth is actually thinking. If the person has already returned to the other world, the spirit can give messages to the people living on earth through Master Okawa.

Since 2009, more than 1,150 sessions of spiritual messages have been openly recorded by Master Okawa, and the majority of these have been published. Spiritual messages from the guardian spirits of people living today such as Donald Trump, former Japanese Prime Minister Shinzo Abe and Chinese President Xi Jinping, as well as spiritual messages sent from the spirit world by Jesus Christ, Muhammad, Thomas Edison, Mother Teresa, Steve Jobs and Nelson Mandela are just a tiny pack of spiritual messages that were published so far.

Domestically, in Japan, these spiritual messages are being read by a wide range of politicians and mass media, and the high-level contents of these books are delivering an impact even more on politics, news and public opinion. In recent years, there have been spiritual messages recorded in English, and English translations are being done on the spiritual messages given in Japanese. These have been published overseas, one after another, and have started to shake the world.

*For more about spiritual messages and a complete list of books in the Spiritual Interview Series, visit **okawabooks.com***

ABOUT HAPPY SCIENCE

Happy Science is a global movement that empowers individuals to find purpose and spiritual happiness and to share that happiness with their families, societies, and the world. With more than 12 million members around the world, Happy Science aims to increase awareness of spiritual truths and expand our capacity for love, compassion, and joy so that together we can create the kind of world we all wish to live in.

Activities at Happy Science are based on the Principles of Happiness (Love, Wisdom, Self-Reflection, and Progress). These principles embrace worldwide philosophies and beliefs, transcending boundaries of culture and religions.

> **Love** teaches us to give ourselves freely without expecting anything in return; it encompasses giving, nurturing, and forgiving.
>
> **Wisdom** leads us to the insights of spiritual truths, and opens us to the true meaning of life and the will of God (the universe, the highest power, Buddha).
>
> **Self-Reflection** brings a mindful, nonjudgmental lens to our thoughts and actions to help us find our truest selves—the essence of our souls—and deepen our connection to the highest power. It helps us attain a clean and peaceful mind and leads us to the right life path.

Progress emphasizes the positive, dynamic aspects of our spiritual growth—actions we can take to manifest and spread happiness around the world. It's a path that not only expands our soul growth, but also furthers the collective potential of the world we live in.

PROGRAMS AND EVENTS

The doors of Happy Science are open to all. We offer a variety of programs and events, including self-exploration and self-growth programs, spiritual seminars, meditation and contemplation sessions, study groups, and book events.

Our programs are designed to:
* Deepen your understanding of your purpose and meaning in life
* Improve your relationships and increase your capacity to love unconditionally
* Attain peace of mind, decrease anxiety and stress, and feel positive
* Gain deeper insights and a broader perspective on the world
* Learn how to overcome life's challenges
  ... and much more.

*For more information, visit **happy-science.org**.*

OUR ACTIVITIES

Happy Science does other various activities to provide support for those in need.

◆ **You Are An Angel! General Incorporated Association**

Happy Science has a volunteer network in Japan that encourages and supports children with disabilities as well as their parents and guardians.

◆ **Never Mind School for Truancy**

At 'Never Mind,' we support students who find it very challenging to attend schools in Japan. We also nurture their self-help spirit and power to rebound against obstacles in life based on Master Okawa's teachings and faith.

◆ **"Prevention Against Suicide" Campaign since 2003**

A nationwide campaign to reduce suicides; over 20,000 people commit suicide every year in Japan. "The Suicide Prevention Website-Words of Truth for You-" presents spiritual prescriptions for worries such as depression, lost love, extramarital affairs, bullying and work-related problems, thereby saving many lives.

◆ **Support for Anti-bullying Campaigns**

Happy Science provides support for a group of parents and guardians, Network to Protect Children from Bullying, a general incorporated foundation launched in Japan to end bullying, including those that can even be called a criminal offense. So far, the network received more than 5,000 cases and resolved 90% of them.

- **The Golden Age Scholarship**

    This scholarship is granted to students who can contribute greatly and bring a hopeful future to the world.

- **Success No.1**
  Buddha's Truth Afterschool Academy

    Happy Science has over 180 classrooms throughout Japan and in several cities around the world that focus on afterschool education for children. The education focuses on faith and morals in addition to supporting children's school studies.

- **Angel Plan V**

    For children under the age of kindergarten, Happy Science holds classes for nurturing healthy, positive, and creative boys and girls.

- **Future Stars Training Department**

    The Future Stars Training Department was founded within the Happy Science Media Division with the goal of nurturing talented individuals to become successful in the performing arts and entertainment industry.

- **New Star Production Co., Ltd.**
  ARI Production Co., Ltd.

    We have companies to nurture actors and actresses, artists, and vocalists. They are also involved in film production.

ABOUT HAPPY SCIENCE MOVIES

BEAUTIFUL LURE *Coming Soon*

STORY With both beauty and wit, Maiko looks for a man who suits her. One night, she finds Taro, a candidate for the prime minister. Everything goes well as she plans, but Taro finds out that she is actually a "Youma", a foxy demon who destroys the country. What does fate hold for them?

For more information, visit ***www.beautifullure.com***

TWICEBORN On VOD NOW

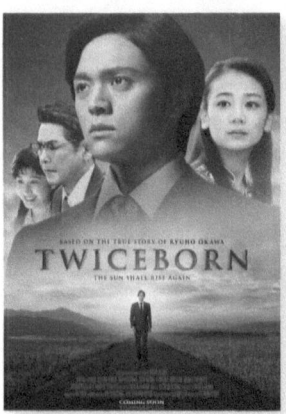

STORY Satoru Ichijo receives a message from the spiritual world and realizes his mission is to lead humankind to happiness. He becomes a successful businessman while publishing spiritual messages secretly, but the devil's temptation shakes his mind and...

41 Awards from 8 Countries!

For more information, visit ***www.twicebornmovie.com***

IMMORTAL HERO `On VOD NOW`

Based on the true story of a man whose near-death experience inspires him to choose life... and change the lives of millions.

42 Awards from 9 Countries!

SPAIN
BARCELONA INTERNATIONAL FILM FESTIVAL 2019
[THE CASTELL AWARDS]

SPAIN
MADRID INTERNATIONAL FILM FESTIVAL 2019
[BEST DIRECTOR OF A FOREIGN LANGUAGE FEATURE FILM]

ITALY
FLORENCE FILM AWARDS JUL 2019
[HONORABLE MENTION: FEATURE FILM]

USA
INDIE VISIONS FILM FESTIVAL JUL 2019 [WINNER (NARRATIVE FEATURE FILM)]

ITALY
FLORENCE FILM AWARDS JUL 2019
[BEST ORIGINAL SCREENPLAY]

ITALY
DIAMOND FILM AWARDS JUL 2019 [WINNER (NARRATIVE FEATURE FILM)]

...and more!

For more information, visit *www.immortal-hero.com*

THE REAL EXORCIST `On VOD NOW`

58 Awards from 9 Countries!

STORY Tokyo —the most mystical city in the world where you find spiritual spots in the most unexpected places. Sayuri works as a part-time waitress at a small coffee shop "Extra" where regular customers enjoy the authentic coffee that the owner brews. Meanwhile, Sayuri uses her supernatural powers to help those who are troubled by spiritual phenomena one after another. Through her special consultations, she touches the hearts of the people and helps them by showing the truths of the invisible world.

USA
GOLD REMI AWARD
53rd WorldFest Houston International Film Festival 2020

MONACO
BEST FEATURE FILM
17th Angel Film Awards 2020
Monaco International Film Festival

NIGERIA
BEST FEATURE FILM
EKO International Film Festival 2020

THAI
BEST PRODUCTION DESIGN
Thai International Film Festival 2020

For more information, visit *www.realexorcistmovie.com*

 **ABOUT HAPPINESS REALIZATION PARTY**

The Happiness Realization Party (HRP) was founded in May 2009 by Master Ryuho Okawa as part of the Happy Science Group to offer concrete and proactive solutions to the current issues such as military threats from North Korea and China and the long-term economic recession. HRP aims to implement drastic reforms of the Japanese government, thereby bringing peace and prosperity to Japan. To accomplish this, HRP proposes two key policies:

1) Strengthening the national security and the Japan-U.S. alliance, which plays a vital role in the stability of Asia.

2) Improving the Japanese economy by implementing drastic tax cuts, taking monetary easing measures and creating new major industries.

HRP advocates that Japan should offer a model of a religious nation that allows diverse values and beliefs to coexist, and that contributes to global peace.

*For more information, visit **en.hr-party.jp***

HAPPY SCIENCE ACADEMY JUNIOR AND SENIOR HIGH SCHOOL

Happy Science Academy Junior and Senior High School is a boarding school founded with the goal of educating the future leaders of the world who can have a big vision, persevere, and take on new challenges.

Currently, there are two campuses in Japan; the Nasu Main Campus in Tochigi Prefecture, founded in 2010, and the Kansai Campus in Shiga Prefecture, founded in 2013.

Nasu Main Campus

Kansai Campus

CONTACT INFORMATION

Happy Science is a worldwide organization with faith centers around the globe. For a comprehensive list of centers, visit the worldwide directory at *happy-science.org*. The following are some of the many Happy Science locations:

UNITED STATES AND CANADA

New York
79 Franklin St., New York, NY 10013
Phone: 212-343-7972
Fax: 212-343-7973
Email: ny@happy-science.org
Website: happyscience-usa.org

Los Angeles
1590 E. Del Mar Blvd., Pasadena, CA 91106
Phone: 626-395-7775
Fax: 626-395-7776
Email: la@happy-science.org
Website: happyscience-usa.org

New Jersey
725 River Rd, #102B, Edgewater, NJ 07020
Phone: 201-313-0127
Fax: 201-313-0120
Email: nj@happy-science.org
Website: happyscience-usa.org

Orange County
10231 Slater Ave., #204
Fountain Valley, CA 92708
Phone: 714-745-1140
Email: oc@happy-science.org
Website: happyscience-usa.org

Florida
5208 8th St., St. Zephyrhills, FL 33542
Phone: 813-715-0000
Fax: 813-715-0010
Email: florida@happy-science.org
Website: happyscience-usa.org

San Diego
7841 Balboa Ave., Suite #202
San Diego, CA 92111
Phone: 626-395-7775
Fax: 626-395-7776
E-mail: sandiego@happy-science.org
Website: happyscience-usa.org

Atlanta
1874 Piedmont Ave., NE Suite 360-C
Atlanta, GA 30324
Phone: 404-892-7770
Email: atlanta@happy-science.org
Website: happyscience-usa.org

Hawaii
Phone: 808-591-9772
Fax: 808-591-9776
Email: hi@happy-science.org
Website: happyscience-usa.org

San Francisco
525 Clinton St.
Redwood City, CA 94062
Phone & Fax: 650-363-2777
Email: sf@happy-science.org
Website: happyscience-usa.org

Kauai
3343 Kanakolu Street, Suite 5
Lihue, HI 96766, U.S.A.
Phone: 808-822-7007
Fax: 808-822-6007
Email: kauai-hi@happy-science.org
Website: happyscience-usa.org

Toronto
845 The Queensway
Etobicoke ON M8Z 1N6 Canada
Phone: 1-416-901-3747
Email: toronto@happy-science.org
Website: happy-science.ca

Vancouver
#201-2607 East 49th Avenue
Vancouver, BC, V5S 1J9, Canada
Phone: 1-604-437-7735
Fax: 1-604-437-7764
Email: vancouver@happy-science.org
Website: happy-science.ca

INTERNATIONAL

Tokyo
1-6-7 Togoshi, Shinagawa
Tokyo, 142-0041 Japan
Phone: 81-3-6384-5770
Fax: 81-3-6384-5776
Email: tokyo@happy-science.org
Website: happy-science.org

Seoul
74, Sadang-ro 27-gil,
Dongjak-gu, Seoul, Korea
Phone: 82-2-3478-8777
Fax: 82-2-3478-9777
Email: korea@happy-science.org
Website: happyscience-korea.org

London
3 Margaret St.
London,W1W 8RE United Kingdom
Phone: 44-20-7323-9255
Fax: 44-20-7323-9344
Email: eu@happy-science.org
Website: happyscience-uk.org

Taipei
No. 89, Lane 155, Dunhua N. Road
Songshan District, Taipei City 105, Taiwan
Phone: 886-2-2719-9377
Fax: 886-2-2719-5570
Email: taiwan@happy-science.org
Website: happyscience-tw.org

Sydney
516 Pacific Hwy, Lane Cove North,
NSW 2066, Australia
Phone: 61-2-9411-2877
Fax: 61-2-9411-2822
Email: sydney@happy-science.org

Malaysia
No 22A, Block 2, Jalil Link Jalan Jalil Jaya 2,
Bukit Jalil 57000, Kuala Lumpur, Malaysia
Phone: 60-3-8998-7877
Fax: 60-3-8998-7977
Email: malaysia@happy-science.org
Website: happyscience.org.my

Brazil Headquarters
Rua. Domingos de Morais 1154,
Vila Mariana, Sao Paulo SP
CEP 04009-002, Brazil
Phone: 55-11-5088-3800
Fax: 55-11-5088-3806
Email: sp@happy-science.org
Website: happyscience.com.br

Nepal
Kathmandu Metropolitan City Ward
No. 15,
Ring Road, Kimdol,
Sitapaila Kathmandu, Nepal
Phone: 97-714-272931
Email: nepal@happy-science.org

Jundiai
Rua Congo, 447, Jd. Bonfiglioli
Jundiai-CEP, 13207-340
Phone: 55-11-4587-5952
Email: jundiai@happy-science.org

Uganda
Plot 877 Rubaga Road, Kampala
P.O. Box 34130, Kampala, Uganda
Phone: 256-79-4682-121
Email: uganda@happy-science.org
Website: happyscience-uganda.org

ABOUT IRH PRESS

IRH Press Co., Ltd., based in Tokyo, was founded in 1987 as a publishing division of Happy Science. IRH Press publishes religious and spiritual books, journals, magazines and also operates broadcast and film production enterprises. For more information, visit *okawabooks.com*.

Follow us on:
Facebook: Okawa Books   **Twitter:** Okawa Books
Goodreads: Ryuho Okawa   **Instagram:** OkawaBooks
Pinterest: Okawa Books

---- **MEDIA** ----

OKAWA BOOK CLUB

A conversation about Ryuho Okawa's titles, topics ranging from self-help, current affairs, spirituality and religions.

Available at iTunes, Spotify and Amazon Music.

Apple iTunes:
https://podcasts.apple.com/us/podcast/okawa-book-club/id1527893043

Spotify:
https://open.spotify.com/show/09mpgX2iJ6stVm4eBRdo2b

Amazon Music:
https://music.amazon.com/podcasts/7b759f24-ff72-4523-bfee-24f48294998f/Okawa-Book-Club

BOOKS BY RYUHO OKAWA

RYUHO OKAWA'S LAWS SERIES

The Laws Series is an annual volume of books that are mainly comprised of Ryuho Okawa's lectures on various topics that highlight principles and guidelines for the activities of Happy Science every year. *The Laws of the Sun*, the first publication of the laws series, ranked in the annual best-selling list in Japan in 1987. Since then, all of the laws series' titles have ranked in the annual best-selling list for more than two decades, setting socio-cultural trends in Japan and around the world.

The 27th Laws Series
THE LAWS OF SECRET
AWAKEN TO THIS NEW WORLD AND CHANGE YOUR LIFE

Hardcover • 258 pages • $22.95
ISBN: 978-1-943869-99-2

Our physical world coexists with the multi-dimensional spirit world and we are constantly interacting with some kind of spiritual energy, whether positive or negative, without consciously realizing it. This book reveals how our lives are affected by invisible influences, including the spiritual reasons behind influenza, the novel coronavirus infection, and other illnesses.

The new view of the world in this book will inspire you to change your life in a better direction, and to become someone who can give hope and courage to others in this age of confusion.

For a complete list of books, visit ***okawabooks.com***

THE TRILOGY

The first three volumes of the Laws Series, *The Laws of the Sun*, *The Golden Laws*, and *The Nine Dimensions* make a trilogy that completes the basic framework of the teachings of God's Truths. *The Laws of the Sun* discusses the structure of God's Laws, *The Golden Laws* expounds on the doctrine of time, and *The Nine Dimensions* reveals the nature of space.

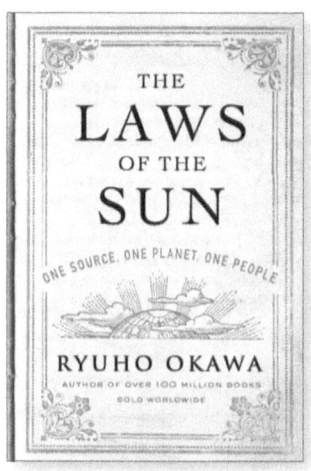

THE LAWS OF THE SUN
ONE SOURCE, ONE PLANET, ONE PEOPLE

Paperback • 288 pages • $15.95
ISBN: 978-1-942125-43-3

IMAGINE IF YOU COULD ASK GOD why He created this world and what spiritual laws He used to shape us— and everything around us. If we could understand His designs and intentions, we could discover what our goals in life should be and whether our actions move us closer to those goals or farther away.

At a young age, a spiritual calling prompted Ryuho Okawa to outline what he innately understood to be universal truths for all humankind. In *The Laws of the Sun*, Okawa outlines these laws of the universe and provides a road map for living one's life with greater purpose and meaning.

In this powerful book, Ryuho Okawa reveals the transcendent nature of consciousness and the secrets of our multidimensional universe and our place in it. By understanding the different stages of love and following the Buddhist Eightfold Path, he believes we can speed up our eternal process of development. *The Laws of the Sun* shows the way to realize true happiness—a happiness that continues from this world through the other.

For a complete list of books, visit **okawabooks.com**

THE GOLDEN LAWS
HISTORY THROUGH THE EYES OF THE ETERNAL BUDDHA
Paperback • 201 pages • $14.95
ISBN: 978-1-941779-81-1

Throughout history, Great Guiding Spirits of Light have been present on Earth in both the East and the West at crucial points in human history to further our spiritual development. *The Golden Laws* reveals how Divine Plan has been unfolding on Earth, and outlines 5,000 years of the secret history of humankind. Once we understand the true course of history, through past, present and into the future, we cannot help but become aware of the significance of our spiritual mission in the present age.

THE NINE DIMENSIONS
UNVEILING THE LAWS OF ETERNITY
Paperback • 168 pages • $15.95
ISBN: 978-0-982698-56-3

This book is a window into the mind of our loving God, who designed this world and the vast, wondrous world of our afterlife as a school with many levels through which our souls learn and grow. When the religions and cultures of the world discover the truth of their common spiritual origin, they will be inspired to accept their differences, come together under faith in God, and build an era of harmony and peaceful progress on Earth.

For a complete list of books, visit **okawabooks.com**

Spiritual Interviews with the Guardian Spirits of Biden and Trump

Paperback • 200 pages • $11.95
ISBN: 978-1-943869-92-3

The 2020 U.S. presidential election will be a turning point in history. In this book, we spiritually closed in on the true thoughts of Biden and Trump to get a forecast of the presidential election. In short, China could become the next hegemonic state if Biden is elected the president. Who you vote for could change people's lives, for better or worse.

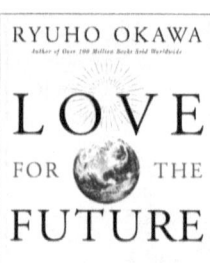

Love for the Future

Building One World of Freedom and Democracy Under God's Truth

Paperback • 312 pages • $15.95
ISBN: 978-1-942125-60-0

This is a compilation of select international lectures given by Ryuho Okawa during his (ongoing) global missionary tours. It espouses freedom and democracy are vital principles to foster peace and shared prosperity, if adopted universally.

On Carbon footprints Reducing

Why Greta gets angry?

Paperback • 135 pages • $11.95
ISBN: 978-1-943869-59-6

Greta Thunberg, a 16-year-old environmental activist from Sweden, gave a speech at the United Nations Climate Actions Summit that shocked the world in September 2019. In this book, Okawa summons the spiritual beings who have influence on Greta, and has them speak their true intention as to why they made her say what she said.

For a complete list of books, visit **okawabooks.com**

BOOKS ON THE NOVEL CORONAVIRUS INFECTION, THE FUTURE PREDICTION TO HUMANKIND

WITH SAVIOR
MESSAGES FROM SPACE BEING YAIDRON

Paperback • 232 pages • $13.95
ISBN: 978-1-943869-94-7

The human race is now faced with multiple unprecedented crises. Perhaps God is warning us humans to reconsider our materialistic and arrogant ways. Fortunately, God has sent us a savior, who is now teaching us to repent and showing us the path we should choose. In this book, space being Yaidron sends his warnings and messages of hope.

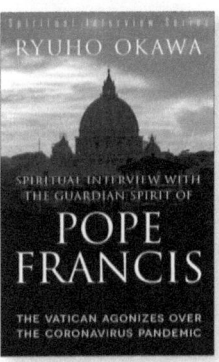

SPIRITUAL INTERVIEW WITH THE GUARDIAN SPIRIT OF POPE FRANCIS
THE VATICAN AGONIZES OVER THE CORONAVIRUS PANDEMIC

Paperback • 268 pages • $13.95
ISBN: 978-1-943869-84-8

In this book, the guardian spirit of Pope Francis confesses his hopelessness, goodwill, and limit as a human being amid the ongoing coronavirus pandemic. Are his prayers heard by Jesus? By also reading *Jesus Christ's Answers to the Coronavirus Pandemic*, you will be able to understand the true will of Jesus and the faith in true God.

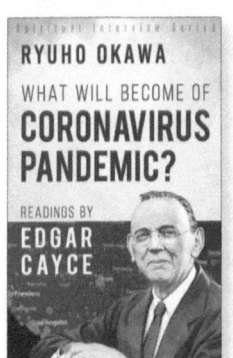

WHAT WILL BECOME OF CORONAVIRUS PANDEMIC?
READINGS BY EDGAR CAYCE

Paperback • 86 pages • $9.95
ISBN: 978-1-943869-82-4

Edgar Cayce, now a spirit in heaven, tells us that the novel coronavirus infection is likely to spread even further, but he also teaches us the truth behind it and how to deal with it. But you, yourself, can gain the power to defeat the novel coronavirus. Here is your light of hope.

For a complete list of books, visit **okawabooks.com**

BOOKS ON THE HIDDEN INTENTION OF WORLD LEADERS

China's Hidden Agenda
The Mastermind Behind the Anti-American and Anti-Japanese Protests

Paperback • 182 pages • $14.95
ISBN: 978-1-937673-18-5

"I wanted to stir up the anti-American movement in the Arab world to make sure that the United States won't be able to attack Syria or Iran…I'm the mastermind behind the Muhammad video."

—Xi Jinping's Guardian Spirit

Hong Kong Revolution
Spiritual Messages of the Guardian Spirits of Xi Jinping and Agnes Chow Ting

Paperback • 282 pages • $13.95
ISBN: 978-1-943869-55-8

The Hong Kong protests that are gathering the attention of the world. What is Xi Jinping plotting? How far is Agnes Chow, the 'Goddess of Democracy,' willing to go? Their guardian spirits reveal issues of conflict in this exciting new book!

Spiritual Messages from the Guardian Spirit of Ayatollah Khamenei and General Soleimani
For the Mutual Understanding between Iran and the U.S.

Paperback • 165 pages • $11.95
ISBN: 978-1-943869-63-3

In January 2020, Soleimani was killed in Iraq. Only a day after the drone attack, his spirit visited Okawa in Tokyo. Chapter 1 is a record of the spiritual session. Chapter 2 is the record of the spiritual session with the guardian spirit of Ayatollah Khamenei who visited three days later.

---

*For a complete list of books, visit **okawabooks.com***

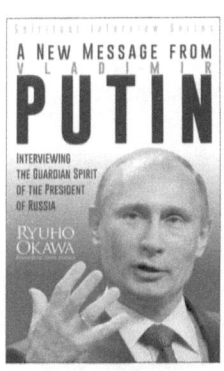

A New Message From Vladimir Putin
Inverviewing the Guardian Spirit of the President of Russia

Paperback • 235 pages • $14.95
ISBN: 978-1-937673-94-9

We hereby bring you the spiritual message from the guardian spirit of President Putin, the politician who is the center of attention of not just the people of Russia but of the whole world, regardless of it being in a good or a bad way. In the Preface, it says, "President Putin's true intentions, which are 90 percent misunderstood."

The New Diplomatic Strategies of Sir Winston Churchill
A Spiritual Interview with the Former Prime Minister Regarding the Age of Perseverance

Paperback • 188 pages • $14.95
ISBN: 978-1-937673-80-2

If there is a chance to hear the opinion of Sir Winston Churchill on current international affairs, journalists around the world will probably be interested to hear this. This book made this possible.

Spiritual Interview with the Guardian Spirit of Angela Merkel
Revealing Her True Intentions, Visions, and Challenges

Paperback • 107 pages • $9.95
ISBN: 978-1-943869-45-9

In this book, Merkel's subconscious speaks on the concept of the EU using extremely theoretical and philosophical words. Read on and you will see why in the latter half of the interview. Chancellor Merkel is the reincarnation of a great German philosopher who had a profound impact on the founding concept of the League of Nations.

*For a complete list of books, visit **okawabooks.com***

BOOKS ON SURVIVING IN THE AGE OF CRISIS

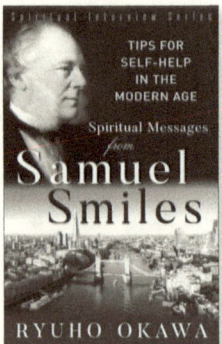

SPIRITUAL MESSAGES FROM SAMUEL SMILES
TIPS FOR SELF-HELP IN THE MODERN AGE

Paperback • 182 pages • $11.95
ISBN: 978-1-943869-69-5

If Smiles was alive today and saw what the world has come to, what would he think and say? What kind of advice would he give to his home country, England, seeing the state it is in over the Brexit issue? The answers to these questions are in this very book.

HOW TO SURVIVE THE CORONAVIRUS RECESSION

Paperback • 171 pages • $14.95
ISBN: 978-1-943869-97-8

From the perspectives of both economics and health, this book delves into how you can survive the coronavirus recession. As taught by the author Ryuho Okawa, there is a strong relationship between your spiritual health and immunity, and he demonstrates the mindset you should have as well as introduces a very effective meditation that you can do to truly strengthen your immunity.

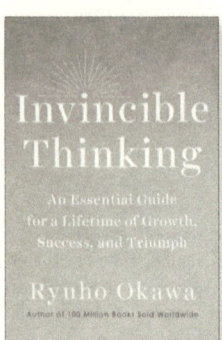

INVINCIBLE THINKING
AN ESSENTIAL GUIDE FOR A LIFETIME OF GROWTH, SUCCESS, AND TRIUMPH

Hardcover • 208 pages • $16.95
ISBN: 978-1-942125-25-9

In this book, Ryuho Okawa lays out the principles of invincible thinking that will allow us to achieve long-lasting triumph. This powerful and unique philosophy is not only about becoming successful or achieving our goal in life, but also about building the foundation of life that becomes the basis of our life-long, lasting success and happiness.

For a complete list of books, visit okawabooks.com

BOOKS ON THE TRUTH OF THE SPIRIT WORLD

THE POSSESSION
KNOW THE GHOST CONDITION AND
OVERCOME NEGATIVE SPIRITUAL INFLUENCE

Paperback • 114 pages • $14.95
ISBN: 978-1-943869-66-4

Possession is neither an exceptional occurrence nor unscientific superstition; it's a phenomenon, based on spiritual principles, that is still quite common in the modern society. Through this book, you can find the way to change your own mind and free yourself from possession, and the way to exorcise devils by relying on the power of angels and God.

HEALING FROM WITHIN
LIFE-CHANGING KEYS TO CALM, SPIRITUAL, AND HEALTHY LIVING

Paperback • 208 pages • $15.95
ISBN:978-1-942125-18-1

None of us wants to become sick, but why is it that we can't avoid illness in life? Is there a meaning behind illness? In this book, author Ryuho Okawa reveals the true causes and remedies for various illnesses that modern medicine doesn't know how to heal. Building a happier and healthier life starts with believing in the power of our mind and understanding the relationship between mind and body.

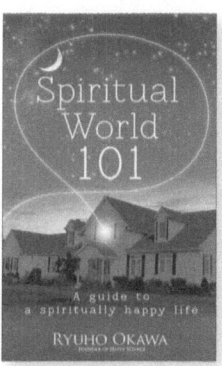

SPIRITUAL WORLD 101
A GUIDE TO A SPIRITUALLY HAPPY LIFE

Paperback • 184 pages • $14.95
ISBN: 978-1-941779-43-9

This book is a spiritual guidebook that will answer all your questions about the spiritual world, with illustrations and diagrams explaining about your guardian spirit and the secrets of God and Buddha. By reading this book, you will be able to understand the true meaning of life and find happiness in everyday life.

---

*For a complete list of books, visit **okawabooks.com***

THE LAWS OF HOPE
The Light is Here

THE HELL YOU NEVER KNEW
and How to Avoid Going There

WORRY-FREE LIVING
Let Go of Stress and Live in Peace and Happiness

THE STRONG MIND
The Art of Building the Inner Strength
to Overcome Life's Difficulties

THE LAWS OF INVINCIBLE LEADERSHIP
An Empowering Guide for Continuous and
Lasting Success in Business and in Life

THE REAL EXORCIST
Attain Wisdom to Conquer Evil

THINK BIG!
Be Positive and Be Brave to Achieve Your Dreams

CHANGE YOUR LIFE, CHANGE THE WORLD
A Spiritual Guide to Living Now

INVITATION TO HAPPINESS
7 Inspirations from Your Inner Angel

---

*For a complete list of books, visit **okawabooks.com***

MUSIC BY RYUHO OKAWA

— THE THUNDER —

a composition for repelling the Coronavirus

CD available at Happy Science local branches and shoja (temples)

We have been granted this music from our Lord. It will repel away the novel Coronavirus originated in China. Experience this magnificent powerful music.

Search on YouTube

the thunder coronavirus

for a short ad!

 Available online
Spotify iTunes Amazon

THE EXORCISM

prayer music for repelling Lost Spirits

CD available at Happy Science local branches and shoja (temples)

Feel the divine vibrations of this Japanese and Western exorcising symphony to banish all evil possessions you suffer from and to purify your space!

Search on YouTube

the exorcism repelling

for a short ad!

 Available online
Spotify iTunes Amazon

www.ingramcontent.com/pod-product-compliance
Lightning Source LLC
Chambersburg PA
CBHW030147100526
44592CB00009B/152